How to Choose a Winning Title

A Guide for Writers, Editors, and Publishers

by Nat G. Bodian

ORYX PRESS
1989

The rare Arabian Oryx is believed to have inspired the myth of the unicorn. This desert antelope became virtually extinct in the early 1960s. At that time several groups of international conservationists arranged to have 9 animals sent to the Phoenix Zoo to be the nucleus of a captive breeding herd. Today the Oryx population is nearly 800, and over 400 have been returned to reserves in the Middle East.

Copyright © 1989 by Nat G. Bodian
Published by The Oryx Press
2214 North Central at Encanto
Phoenix, Arizona 85004-1483

Published simultaneously in Canada

Printed and Bound in the United States of America

∞ The paper used in this publication meets the minimum requirements of American National Standard for Information Science—Permanence of Paper for Printed Library Materials, ANSI Z39.48, 1984.

Library of Congress Cataloging-in-Publication Data

Bodian, Nat G., 1921–
    How to choose a winning title : a guide for writers, editors, and publishers / by Nat G. Bodian.
        p. cm.
    Includes index.
    ISBN 0-89774-540-X
    1. Titles of books.   2. Publishers and publishing.   I. Title.
PN171.T5B64 1988
808'.02—dc 19   88-25235

CONTENTS

PREFACE

In July 1987, while a scheduled speaker at the 20th National Meeting of COSMEP, the International Association of Small Publishers, on the UCLA campus, I was invited to evaluate and give opinions on the titles of a number of books issued by attending publishers.

At the conclusion of my remarks, I was inundated with requests from attendees for opinions on specific titles of their books, and I attempted off-the-cuff judgments as time permitted.

I was surprised at the degree of random or poor judgment some small press publishers had shown in their titling efforts, making it relatively easy to suggest improvements for a number of the samples offered. When the titles were weak or passive, I was able to suggest minor modifications right away to strengthen them from a marketing standpoint. In a few instances, titles had been whimsically chosen and bore no relationship to the subject or content of the book. In such cases, I asked for a short explanation of what the book was about, and the publisher's own words in the explanation suggested a more appropriate or better title.

The problems I encountered that day at UCLA are not limited to small press publishers. My own experience and subsequent research on book titling indicates that larger publishing establishments also frequently issue books that demonstrate considerable weakness or inappropriateness in title selection.

"Title selection," as one publisher told me, "is an agonizing experience." At John Wiley & Sons, Inc., over the span of 12 years as a book marketer, I'd seen the same thing happen with numerous manuscript titles. It is surprising how authors who are highly regarded scientists, engineers, educators, or authorities in their fields, and who have crafted brilliant works, sometimes turn them in to their publishers with highly inappropriate titles.

I found it not unusual, from discussions over the years with authors, to learn that eminent scholars and scientists admit to soliciting the help of spouses and children in title selection and have submitted works with titles considered to be cute or catchy rather than practical. Weak title selection is, apparently, a common practice among both the high and the humble.

While I had repeatedly encountered titling problems throughout my nearly 30 years in the book industry, it had not previously occurred to me that anything could be done about it. But the 1987 meeting at UCLA proved to be the catalyst.

On my return to New York from that meeting, I reflected on the intense hunger of COSMEP publishers for titling guidance and on my own experience in overcoming titling problems during my career as a publishing marketer. The message that came through was clear: A need exists for comprehensive and detailed guidelines to aid in creating, selecting, and shaping appropriate titles for books.

I realized, too, that improper book titling is not by design, but rather from lack of enlightenment. My own experience had indicated that those concerned with titling—whether authors, editors, or publishers—once turned on to the value and effectiveness of good book titles, and provided with samples or examples of related successful works, usually had considerably greater success with subsequent titling efforts.

Only one further step remained before my decision to write this book—a check of Bowker's *Subject Guide to Books in Print*. An entry, "Titles of Books," existed, but only as a cross-reference to something else; the subject of titling as a complete work did not exist in the literature!

This provided the final impetus, and I plunged into a writing assignment that proved to be one of the most unique and demanding challenges of a long career as a publishing marketer and communications professional. You hold in your hands the end result.

In this manual I have tried to cover the subject in depth through interviews with authorities on the topics covered, through extensive research of the literature, and by drawing on my own experience of nearly 30 years as a book marketer and as an author of seven previously published books on book marketing and marketing-related topics.

This guide has been created to provide a helping hand for writers, editors, and publishers, and to assist them in achieving the full potential of advertising, publicity, sales, and public acceptance for their published works through proper title selection. I sincerely hope that *How to Choose a Winning Title* will not only fill a void in the literature, but also serve as guide, companion, and source of ideas and inspiration to all who write, labor with, or produce the printed word.

Nat Bodian
Cranford, New Jersey

INTRODUCTION

While choosing a winning title is of vital concern to writers, editors, publishers, and virtually everyone connected with the written word, no one, my research indicates, has ever before attempted to tackle so difficult a subject in depth.

A few authors have dealt with various specific aspects of titling, and these rather limited efforts have been important contributions in the areas covered. Many of these efforts have been noted and quoted with permission in the various chapters of this work.

But the final decision to undertake such a challenging assignment, as I have noted earlier in the Preface, came when I discovered that no single book existed that treated the subject of titling in a comprehensive and authoritative manner.

GETTING THE PROJECT STARTED

The project started during the summer of 1987, when I spoke to dozens of colleagues at Wiley and to scores of other friends and acquaintances throughout the industry explaining my intention to write an in-depth work that would touch on every aspect of book titling.

In almost every instance I got one of two reactions. The first was wholehearted enthusiasm and encouragement that I proceed; the second was skepticism—such as "Where are you going to find enough material to fill an entire book?"

However, as these reactions became an established pattern, I would follow-up with two questions. More often than not, I got useful answers that were ultimately transformed into solid contributions to this project.

The first question I would ask was "Have you personally had any experience involving a title that you'd like to tell me about?" Many of those I questioned had, and their responses were carefully noted.

The second question I would ask was "Is there anyone you know in publishing or a related field that you think might have a special experience involving a book title or that you think might have some thoughts on titling in general?"

This second question provided dozens of leads, which were faithfully tracked down and often produced useful material. The people I contacted invariably indicated great enthusiasm for this project and, in turn, provided me with names of other individuals I should contact.

From this activity alone, perhaps a third or more of this book was derived—either from direct questions to publishing colleagues, or from pursuing leads provided by them.

Dimi Berkner, former vice president for new business and market development at The Oryx Press, was extremely helpful. After learning of this titling project, she continuously fed me names of librarians, jobbers, editors, book marketers, authors, and others among her vast acquaintanceship who she thought would be useful sources of information. Almost without exception, they proved to be excellent information suppliers, since Dimi had prepared them for my calls and they either had stories to tell or else were quick to provide me with names of others I might be able to interview.

An interesting sidelight of this titling work is that many of those I talked to became so enthusiastic about the project that they initiated their own searches for contacts I might follow-up. Many got back to me two or more times with suggestions and ideas.

Prominent among the many who provided this help were Robert Polhemus, former executive publisher at John Wiley & Sons; Charles Smith, vice president and publisher of the Professional and Reference Division of Macmillan Company; Ben Russak (former head of American Elsevier Publishing Company) of Crane, Russak & Company; and Howard Cady, editorial consultant for William Morrow & Company.

Many Wiley editors provided help, guidance, and support. I'd like to single out for special attention Mary Conway, David Eckroth, Theodore Hoffman, Michael Hamilton, Jacquline Kroschwitz, John Mahaney, Herb Reich, Beatrice Shube, James M. Smith, and George Telecki.

Librarians, as a group, were perhaps the most vocal on titling attitudes and opinions and as enthusiastic about this project as those in the publishing community. Among the numerous librarians who were helpful, I want to give special thanks to Richard Stern, director of the business library at Seton Hall University, and Debra Kaufman, director of the Perkin Elmer libraries, both of whom provided valuable information and leads. Helen Witsenhausen, director of the Wiley corporate library, provided leads and showed me how to use the Bowker *Books in Print* database on CD-ROM for title searches.

For help with the chapters on dictionary titling (Chapter 6) and encyclopedia titling (Chapter 7), I am particularly indebted to Sidney Landau, former editor-in-chief at Funk & Wagnalls and more recently editor-in-chief for the widely acclaimed 3,200-page *International Dictionary of Medicine and Biology* (Wiley, 1986), and to Martin Grayson, editor-in-chief of the classic Third Edition of the *Kirk-Othmer Encyclopedia of Chemical Technology* (Wiley, 1985), and currently president and publisher at VCH Publishers, Inc. Both provided valuable insights that made these two chapters possible and, even more, encouragement and warm support during the entire time this book was being written.

In preparing Chapter 21, "Title Construction, Punctuation, and Design: The Technical End," my own personal references were augmented by more than a dozen publishing style guides supplied mainly by the editorial and production staffs at Wiley, by David Schulbaum of the American Chemical Society, and by The University of Chicago Press.

For "Fiction and General Nonfiction" (Chapter 1), "Business and Professional Books" (Chapter 2), "Travel Guides and Books, Cookbooks, and Art Books" (Chapter 8), "Religious Books" (Chapter 9), and "Children's Books" (Chapter 10), I obtained numerous leads and a liberal education on the titling of all these book types from a painstaking review of 1980s back issues of *Publishers Weekly*, along with selected back issues of *The Bookseller, Choice, Library Journal,* and *Small Press.*

For reasons I have never been able to understand, relatively few among the giants in the publishing industry who help bring forth the printed word are themselves authors of publishing-related works. When they do take pen (or word processor) in hand, their efforts are usually of exceptional quality.

Among the publishing industry "prominents" who have created enduring guides and given their support and encouragement to this work, I would like to cite some who have given me permission to include segments, excerpts, or adaptations of their words. These include Robert A. Day for permission to use material from his third edition of *How to Write and Publish a Scientific Paper* (Oryx Press, 1988), Daniel Fischel for permission to adapt material from *A Practical Guide to Writing and Publishing Professional Books* (Van Nostrand Reinhold, 1984), Scott Meredith for permission to quote his words in *Writing to Sell* (Harper & Row, 1984), and finally to Tom and Marilyn Ross for their permission to quote from *The Complete Guide to Self-Publishing* (Writer's Digest Books, 1985).

Aside from my own considerable titling experience at Wiley, another extremely helpful source of titling information and outlook came from the numerous authors of Wiley books and encyclopedias with whom my work as manager of special projects brought me in contact. In the course of conversations with these authors—mainly scholars and scientists—most shared with me their own views on titling and often their own agonies in the titling of their numerous published works.

INFORMATION LOCALES

Aside from interviews in person, by telephone, and by mail, one of the most useful information sources was my personal publishing library, developed over nearly 30 years in the publishing industry, and greatly enhanced during the past decade as a reference center for my earlier written works, which now number seven published books, primarily on publishing-marketing topics, and over 35 articles for the publishing industry press.

Two other sources of information in my local community of Cranford, New Jersey, were the Cranford Public Library and the library of the Union County College, where I went through scores of books and periodicals on writing and authorship.

There were also a number of unlikely information locales that provided material for many of the pages that follow. One such unlikely locale was a book fair in the middle of Fifth Avenue, New York City, held each summer under the banner "New York is Book Country."

Here, in the middle of Fifth Avenue, usually one of the busiest avenues in New York City, and armed only with pad and pencil, reminiscent of my earlier career as a newspaper reporter, I was able to interview on the spot a number of currently prominent authors and to retell their titling experiences on the pages that follow.

Other unlikely locales that provided tips and leads for this book included the elevators in the Wiley building at 605 Third Avenue in New York City, a bus, an airplane, and a Union, New Jersey, health club. The latter encounter involved a chat with fellow club member Herman Roth, father of novelist Philip Roth.

This is not a book that wrote itself. Rather, it was a labor, but a labor of love. The challenge was both exciting and stimulating. Many nights, after recording that day's notes on paper, I'd lie sleepless half the night rethinking and rehashing in my thoughts the accomplishments of the day just past and the challenges and possibilities of the day ahead. It was, for the most part, a fact-finding quest, drawn from many different sources, and carefully assembled in bits and pieces and woven together into the comprehensive work that follows.

CHAPTER 1

FICTION AND GENERAL NONFICTION

✓ CHOOSING A TITLE: GENERAL GUIDELINES*

Choose a title for your book at least as carefully as you would select a given name for your first-born child. In making the choice, work closely with your editor or publisher, who will be concerned with factors perhaps not familiar to you, such as marketing and advertising.

Try a distinctive title or at least one not close to that of a competing work still in print. If possible, your title should be informative; bear in mind the advantages of key words for computer-based bibliographers and for indexing. It should be easy to refer to in speech even if in a shortened or casual form.

Generally speaking, you should keep the title short. There is nothing wrong with adding a subtitle even if it is of considerable length. But it may not be wise to strain too hard to make the title fully and accurately reflect the content. *War and Peace* and *The Origin of Species* have done well despite brevity.

Every year hundreds of authors begin their book titles with *Introduction to*, thereby sentencing them to burial among their fellow introductions in card catalogs and reference books. . . . So avoid words like *Introduction, Beginning,* and *Selected*, at least at the beginning of your title.

In *The Art of Plain Talk* (Harper & Row, 1946), Rudolph Flesch says that "to reach an audience at a certain level of reading . . . you not only have to talk the kind of language they will be able to understand without effort, but ordinarily you have to go one step below that level to be sure your ideas will get across."

In choosing a title for your book, you must consider the level of your audience and present the title in a language your intended readership will understand. There are various levels of book title readability. In descending order of complexity and reading difficulty, the following scheme applies:

---

*Portions adapted from *Into Print: A Practical Guide to Writing, Illustrating and Publishing* by Mary Hill and Wendell Cochran, 1977. Used by permission of William Kaufmann, Inc., 95 First Street, Los Altos, CA 94022.

1. Titles for scientific and professional audiences.
2. Titles for academic audiences.
3. Titles for the general reading public.
4. Titles designed to provide entertainment or cater to hobbies/ personal interests.
5. Titles that cater to children.

✓ A PUBLIC LIBRARIAN'S VIEWS

"I think a lot about a book's title because the title can help sell the book to browsers, either because it is intriguing, or because it helps tell what the book is about. This is particularly true of science fiction or mystery books where an intriguing title is very important."

The comment is from Nora Wallenson of the Baltimore Public Library, who continues:

"One particular problem we have at the Baltimore Public Library is with similar titles. Almost every season there are two or three popular titles that are similar to one another. This leads to scrambled title requests. We have to be aware of these titles and their differences so we can interpret these requests and direct inquirers to the right title.

"A real turnoff for me is nonfiction books with vague titles. It can be very irritating when you order a book with a title you think is about a particular subject and then inspect the book and find that it is about something entirely different."

✓ VIEWS FROM THE HEAD OF A LEADING LITERARY AGENCY*

"A book's title," says Scott Meredith, head of one of the country's largest literary agencies, "is an important part of your sales campaign. Provided your manuscript is neat and attractively prepared, it is the first thing the editor notices."

"Avoid the dull or trite title," Meredith advises. "It repels rather than attracts the reader because it makes him suspect the story itself will be just as dull or trite."

"Old saws, overworked proverbs, famous quotations from the Bible, very popular song titles—any phrases at all which have become trite through too common usage are sure to make trite titles," adds Meredith.

"There are exceptions when proverbs, sayings, and quotations can make good titles—when they're familiar enough to be recognized, but

---

*Reprinted by permission of the Scott Meredith Literary Agency, Inc., 845 Third Avenue, New York, NY 10022.

not so familiar as to be trite, as in *The Naked and the Dead,* when triteness is canceled out by an amusing or interesting twist."

Meredith, in *Writing to Sell* (Harper & Row, 1960), describes how detective-story writers have developed the knack of twisting trite phrases into fresh and interesting titles. He cites such examples as:

✦ *Let Me Kill You, Sweetheart*
✦ *The Facts of Death*
✦ *Dead Ernest*
✦ *Has Anyone Here Slain Kelly?*
✦ *Just Around the Coroner*
✦ *The Quack and the Dead*
✦ *Grave and a Haircut*

"Avoid titles," admonishes Meredith, "that sound misleading. The title should not sound like one kind of a story if you are offering another. A love story with a dude ranch locale should not have a title such as *Blazing Guns* that might imply it was a western.

"*The Lost Weekend* was perfect for the book because it conveyed perfectly the mood of the story.

"Books have been published under perfectly foul titles which have done very well anyhow. However, when your by-line on a manuscript does not automatically signal that your story is a good one, little things are sometimes enough to tip the scales against you. The first bad impression made by a poor title may be just enough to keep a reader from dipping into the manuscript by a name unknown, when otherwise he might read and enjoy it and write a glowing report to the editor."

Concludes Meredith: "It isn't much more effort to get a good title instead of settling for a bad one, so you might as well do it right."

✔ TITLING FOR SELF-PUBLISHERS

Planning to publish yourself? Tom and Marilyn Ross* offer this sound advice on titling: "Christen it with a zesty title. The best ones are brief—certainly no more than six words and preferably two or three, descriptive and lively."

The Rosses then cite an exception to their rule: *If Life Is a Bowl of Cherries, What Am I Doing in the Pits?* and add "Yes, this one is more than six words, but when you reach Erma Bombeck's status, you can break the rules, too."

---

*Adapted from *The Complete Guide to Self-Publishing* by Tom and Marilyn Ross, Cincinnati: Writer's Digest Books, 1985. Used by permission of the authors.

"Sometimes a play on words can have a dramatic effect," say the Rosses. Capitalizing on the vastly popular *What Color Is Your Parachute?* Price/Stern/Sloan came out with *What Color Is Your Parody?*

"There are also some negatives to avoid," the Rosses say, "trite phrases such as 'All That Glitters Is Not Gold' or 'Mother's Little Helper' or 'To Be or Not to Be'. Also avoid profane or controversial titles that will give potential readers a chance to dislike your book on sight.

"If you're titling a fiction work, sometimes an object or living thing told about the book lends itself to appropriate symbolism to stand for the whole book. Two examples of this method are *The Thornbirds* and *Valley of the Dolls.*

"Sometimes with a switch of words you can communicate a sense of mystery as did Mary Stewart with her *Touch Not the Cat.* If she had titled it *Don't Touch the Cat*, the title would have lost that charm and mystery."

✓ A USEFUL REFERENCE SOURCE FOR NONFICTION TRADE TITLES

"I have found books of quotations to be invaluable sources for nonfiction trade titles." The speaker is Charles E. Smith, vice-president and publisher of Macmillan Publishing Company and a seasoned professional with a long string of successes.

"For a work on the scientists who made modern astronomy, I found an interesting passage from Milton's *Paradise Lost.* A portion of the passage went like this:

Into this wild abyss the ware Fiend
Stood on the brink of Hell and looked a while,
Pondering his voyage; for no narrow frith
He had to cross.

The work was published as *This Wild Abyss: The Story of the Men Who Made Modern Astronomy.* It was a very successful trade title."

✓ THE TITLE AS MINI-ADVERTISEMENT FOR THE BOOK

The titles of popular books on business and investment provide a lesson on how the title of a book can serve as a mini-advertisement, even in the absence of supporting descriptive matter: the title must make the essence of the book come alive for its intended audience. Meaningful titles are not limited to any one area; the rule can be applied to any book. Here are examples of ways that a book title can be shaped to give it meaning:

✦ Title describing content: *Fundamentals of Advertising Research*

✦ Title identifying audience: *The Chemist's Companion*

✦ Title stressing completeness: *Comprehensive Review of Medical Technology*

✦ Title providing an industry standard: *IEEE Standard Test Procedures for Antennas*

✦ Title promising a benefit: *How to Write Articles that Sell*

✦ Title showing level of content: *Introduction to Computer Programming*

✦ Title stressing regional coverage: *Bed and Breakfast Homes in Southern California*

✦ Title covering a specific time period: *A Day in the Life of America*

✦ Title covering a broad field: *Encyclopedia of Science and Technology*

✦ Title solving a problem: *What to Do When the Taxman Calls*

✦ Title offering fast results: *The One-Minute Manager*

✓ THE HITCH-YOUR-WAGON-TO-A-STAR TECHNIQUE

❝. . . give someone else's concept an entirely new twist.**❞**
—*William A. Cohen*
Building a Mail Order Business (Wiley, 1984)

When the title of a successful book takes an offbeat approach or uses uncommon words or phrasing, it is often quickly followed by a flurry of sound-alike titles.

When *How to Flatten Your Stomach* by coach Jim Everroad reached the top of the bestseller lists with over 200,000 copies sold, *How to Flatten Your Tush* by coach Marge Reardon quickly followed and went on to become a bestseller in its own right.

A big winner of the early 1980s was *The One-Minute Manager*, in which authors Kenneth Blanchard and Spencer Johnson converted their business expertise into a runaway bestseller. As it dominated the bestseller lists in 1983–84, others began to "hitch their wagons" to the "One-Minute" phenomenon, as these selected examples from 1983 indicate:

- *The One-Minute Father* by Spencer Johnson
- *The One-Minute Mother* by Spencer Johnson
- *The One-Minute Lover* by Minnie Wiener

In 1984, as *Manager* continued on *The New York Times* bestseller list for a second full year, there appeared:

- *Putting the One-Minute Manager to Work* by Kenneth Blanchard and Robert Lorber
- *The One-Minute Methodology* by Ken Orr
- *The One-Minute Salesperson* by Spencer Johnson
- *The One-Minute Business Lesson* by Charles Bury
- And an enterprising effort to beat the "minute," *The Fifty-Nine Second Employee* by Rae Andre

In 1985–86, with *Manager* still a top seller, more authors joined the "Minute" bandwagon with such titles as:

- *One-Minute Bible Stories*
- *One-Minute Teacher*

Following the concept of giving someone else's concept a new twist, there appeared in 1986 *The Sixty-Second Shiatzu*.

At the end of 1983, there were 30 books in print starting with the words "One-Minute."

The "one-minute" phenomenon in book titling led to time variations, with titles ranging from 59 seconds to 30 minutes and more, such as:

- *The Five-Minute Interview*
- *Six-Minute Souffle*
- *The Fifteen Minute Investor*
- *Thirty-Minute Panorama of the Bible*
- *The Sixty-Minute Flower Gardener*

The "one-minute" magic, however, did not work for every publisher. The *One-Minute Scolding*, issued in 1985, had, by 1987, been reissued as *Who's the Boss? Love, Authority and Parenting.*

✓ SOUND-ALIKE TITLES: LEGALITIES AND COINCIDENCES

Do publishers who hitch their wagons to superstar titles invite legal problems? Apparently not, when it is done frequently and by many.

Harriet Pilpul and Theodora Zavin deal with this question in their book *Rights and Writers* (Dutton, 1960): "Sometimes a title that has been used previously is made safe for subsequent use by the fact that it has been used, not once, but many times before, and the courts are not likely, therefore, to find that the particular word or combination of words is associated in the public mind with any one work."

Then, too, there are sound-alike titles that happen by coincidence and are not created to imitate or follow earlier successes. A striking example is these two 1987 titles:

✦ *When Battered Women Kill*
✦ *Battered Women Who Kill*

The year 1980 was great for coincidences in title similarities. Despite the fact that 15 editions of Charles Dickens's *Great Expectations* were in print, five other books titled *Great Expectations* were published in the fall of that year. Fortunately, each of the 1980 *Great Expectations* had a unique subtitle that made clear their widely differing subjects. A subsequent survey of the two leading trade book wholesalers indicated that there had been no order duplication problems among the various titles.

✔ ALTERNATIVE TO "HITCH-YOUR-WAGON": THE PARODY TITLE

An alternative to the hitch-your-wagon-to-a-star technique is the parody title of a universally recognized work, which capitalizes on the name and fame of the work being parodied. A good example is *White's Law Dictionary*. The Warner Books promotional copy to the book trade called it "a hilarious parody of the universally recognized legal dictionary, *Black's Law Dictionary*," and went on to describe it as a "lexicon of legal terminology [including] entries from *Ambulance Chasing* ('client development') to ZZZ's ('the last word in legal research and writing')."

✔ TYING A TRADE SEQUEL TO ITS PREDECESSOR

Popular trade sequels tend to do well. Because many bookbuyers tend to favor books by authors whom they know and like,* a sequel has a ready-made audience.

---

*Some indication of the sales appeal of sequels may be derived from a Gallup Survey, reported in *Publishers Weekly* (November 23, 1984), in which 16% of the book buyers polled indicated they rarely buy a book by an unfamiliar author, while another 22% said this was "somewhat true."

Sequel titles are often made to sound like their predecessors or show continuity in other ways. Some examples include:

◆ Original: *Hollywood Wives* by Jackie Collins
◆ Sequel: *Hollywood Husbands*
◆ Originals: *North and South* and *Love and War* by John Jakes
◆ Sequel: *Heaven and Hell*
◆ Original: *Free to Be . . . You and Me* by Marlo Thomas and Friends
◆ Sequel: *Free to Be . . . a Family*
◆ Original: *Up the Organization* by Robert Townsend
◆ Sequel: *Further Up the Organization*
◆ Original: *Prizzi's Honor* by Richard Condon
◆ Sequel: *Prizzi's Family*

An added advantage is that authors find sequels easier than new works, since the setting and characters are already well developed and extending a previously told tale is, as a rule, much easier than beginning a new one.

✔ BOLSTERING A NOVEL'S TITLE WITH A COVER ENDORSEMENT

Because the titles of many novels do not by themselves carry enough *sell* to stimulate a purchase, many publishers of popular fiction solicit, in advance of publication, an endorsement from a celebrity or recognized authority and then feature it prominently on the book cover or jacket (occasionally giving it equal prominence with the title) and in advertising.

Morris Philipson, author of the 1987 novel *Somebody Else's Life* and director of the University of Chicago Press, commented on one specific example of this practice (in *Scholarly Publishing*, July 1987): "The one sentence which Graham Greene gave to [*The Spy Who Came in From the Cold*], his judgment that 'This is the best spy story I have ever read,' must have been worth about $5 million of the success of that book alone."

✔ PATTERNS AND IDIOSYNCRASIES IN AUTOBIOGRAPHICAL WORKS

For famous persons, often the name by itself, or the name with a short subtitle, is more than adequate.

In *Books in Print*, there are perhaps 75 or more autobiographical works that are either titled *My Life* or that start with *My Life . . .*, such as *My Life in Music* or *My Life and Times*.

However, for all the easily identifiable autobiographies, there are many more that tend to ramble, contain an insider meaning that few understand, or have no real relationship with the subject of the book. A good case in point is Robert M. Pirsig's *Zen and the Art of Motorcycle Maintenance: An Inquiry into Values*.

Says Marcia Romanansky, director of public library marketing at Baker & Taylor, a leading library supplier, "Here is a book whose title is misleading. *Zen and the Art of Motorcycle Maintenance* is really an autobiography. Sounds like technology from Jack Kerouac."

Consider, too, the 1987 business autobiography by an author with exceptional credentials and an impressive story to tell, but one that tried to get too much, in our opinion, into the three-part title: *Odyssey: Pepsi to Apple . . . The Journey of a Marketing Impressario*. This account by a giant of business, John Sculley, would have been more appealing with a simpler title: perhaps "Wisdom of a Marketing Impressario" or "John Sculley . . . from Pepsi to Apple," or "Odyssey: Journey of a Marketing Impressario."

✔ A SHORT EXPLANATION OF SEXIST AND NONSEXIST LANGUAGE

"There is imperfect agreement today," says Rosalie Maggio in *The Nonsexist Word Finder: A Dictionary of Gender-Free Usage*, published in 1987 by Oryx Press, "on which words are sexist and on what constitutes an adequate substitute for those that are." She defines sexist language as "language that promotes and maintains attitudes that stereotype people according to gender. It assumes that the male is the norm—the significant gender.

"Nonsexist language," counters Ms. Maggio, is "language that treats all people equally and either does not refer to a person's sex at all when it is irrelevant or refers to men and women in symmetrical ways when their gender is relevant."

Ms. Maggio favors gender-free terms "that do not indicate sex and can be used for either men or women, boys or girls." She makes a clear distinction between generic terms and false generics.

Ms. Maggio defines a generic term as "an all-purpose, gender-free word that includes everybody. Examples of generic nouns: *workers, immigrants, people, voters, civilians, church members, elementary school students*." She defines a false generic as "a word that is claimed to include all people, but in reality does not. Examples: *man, mankind, chairman, forefathers, brotherhood, alumni*."

The author was curious as to how author Maggio would treat *forefathers* in her fascinating dictionary—the most comprehensive work of its kind we have seen and great fun to read. She comes up with these alternates: "*ancestor, forerunner, forebear, predecessor, precurser; forefather* and *foremother* if used gender-fairly."

✔ AVOIDING SEXIST LANGUAGE IN BOOK TITLES

Increasingly, publishers of serious nonfiction are avoiding book titles containing sexist language. A few houses have official guidelines on what is and is not considered sexist. In others, the matter is left up to the alertness and sensitivities of the editors involved, who are increasingly likely to be women.

The Prentice-Hall *Author's Guide* addresses the subject of sexist language in its instructions to authors. "Where possible," advises the *Guide*, "refer to people in terms that have no sexual connotations. . . . Try to avoid the use of the word *he* or *man* in the generic sense . . . treat men and women impersonally in regard to occupation, marital status, physical abilities, attitudes, interests, and so on."

McGraw-Hill indicated its concern over the use of sexist language in all of its publications by issuing, in 1974, a book for editors and authors titled *Guidelines for Equal Treatment of the Sexes in McGraw-Hill Book Company Publications.* One of the suggestions made in the manual was avoidance of the word *mankind* and its replacement by such words as *people, humanity, human beings, human race, humankind.*

"One way to avoid sexism in a title," according to Morton S. Freeman, former director of publications for the American Law Institute-American Bar Association (ALI-ABA), "is by writing in the plural" (in *A Treasury for Word Lovers*, Philadelphia: ISI Press, 1983). Instead of: *101 Ways for a Doctor to Expand His Practice,* consider: *101 Ways for Doctors to Expand Their Practices.*

✔ TITLE LENGTH: A YEAR'S BESTSELLING HARDCOVERS

The unwritten rule that the most successful fiction hardcover books have very short titles held for 1986, based on the bestseller list in the March 13, 1987, *Publishers Weekly.*

The top 15 hardcover fiction titles had an average title length of 2.66 words.* Three were only one word long—*It, Wanderlust,* and *Cyclops.* The only two-word title in the top 15 was *Hollywood Husbands.* Six others were three words long; the remaining five titles were four words long.

The top 15 hardcover nonfiction titles, requiring more words, had an average title length of 4.7 words. There was a single one-word title: *Fatherhood,* which ranked first. Four books had compound or two-part titles.† In three of these the parts were separated by a colon; in the fourth, by a dash. Of the four compound titles, two had one word and two had two words in the first part.

Many of the nonfiction titles carried a built-in selling message that defied compactness, for example, *Callanetics: Ten Years Younger in Ten Hours.*

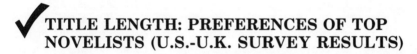

✓ TITLE LENGTH: PREFERENCES OF TOP NOVELISTS (U.S.-U.K. SURVEY RESULTS)

In 1983 the *London Sunday Times* polled its readers for their choice of the top 12 novels written in English since 1945. Simultaneously, *Publishers Weekly* polled its U.S. readers for a like selection and matched its findings with those of the *London Times* in its January 29, 1984 issue.

An interesting finding of the twin surveys is in the length of the titles selected. The average title length in the *Times* poll, including such words as *A* and *The,* was 2.75 words, contrasted with 2.83 words for the *PW* poll.

The U.K. top 12 had 2 one-word titles, 3 two-word titles, 4 three-word titles, 2 four-word titles, and 1 five-word title.

The U.S. top 12 had 2 one-word titles, 3 two-word titles, 4 three-word titles, 1 four-word title, and 2 five-word titles.

Conclusion: For top novels, short titles were the overwhelming preference of such authors as Saul Bellow, Anthony Burgess, Ralph Ellison, John Fowles, Joseph Heller, Vladimir Nabokov, George Orwell, and Thomas Pynchon. None of their selected titles was longer than two words.

---

* In the *PW* list of the bestselling 1987 fiction, average length for the 12 titles chosen was 2.5 words (*PW*, January 8, 1988).

† In the *PW* list of the bestselling 1987 nonfiction, 11 of the 12 titles chosen were compound titles (*PW*, January 8, 1988).

✓ THE COMMON THREAD IN CLASSIC BESTSELLERS

Classic bestsellers over the past several centuries have demonstrated a single common thread: simple titles. Among the all-time bestsellers are such books as:

- ✦ *Ben-Hur*
- ✦ *Gone with the Wind*
- ✦ *How to Win Friends and Influence People*
- ✦ *Ivanhoe*
- ✦ *Mother Goose*
- ✦ *Shakespeare's Plays*
- ✦ *Uncle Tom's Cabin*

Robert Gunning, father of the formula for evaluating clear writing (the "fog index"), looks at some of the all-time bestselling titles of the first half of this century (in *The Technique of Clear Writing, Revised Edition*, New York: McGraw-Hill, 1968) and indicates the reading level of the title:

Title	Reading Level
Peyton Place by Grace Metalious	5th grade
The Carpetbaggers by Harold Robbins	5th grade
To Kill a Mockingbird by Harper Lee	5th grade
I, the Jury by Mickey Spillane	5th grade
The Big Kill by Mickey Spillane	5th grade
God's Little Acre by Erskine Caldwell	6th grade
Gone with the Wind by Margaret Mitchell	6th grade
Exodus by Leon Uris	6th grade
How to Win Friends and Influence People by Dale Carnegie	7th grade
Baby and Child Care by Benjamin Spock	8th grade

✓ TITLE STRUCTURE AND PATTERNS IN BIOGRAPHIES

Biographers, as a group, tend to favor compound titles (i.e., two-part titles, usually separated by a colon) over simple ones, as shown by the biographies listed in a roundup of forthcoming works for 1988 of 125 publishers in *Publishers Weekly*, January 15, 1988. Of the 365 biographies listed, 215, or 59 percent, bore compound titles.

Simple titles ranged in length from one to nine words. Most prominent word lengths were: one-word title, 12; six-word, 11; nine-word, 3; seven- and eight-word, 2 each. The shortest, simplest title: Scribner's *Golda*. Compound titles usually had more words after the colon than before it. Titles with one word before the colon ranged in overall length from 3 words to 12 words. Most had 2 or 3 words after the colon; they made up 23 percent of the compound title total.

Compound titles with 2 words before the colon ranged in overall length from 3 words to 18 words. Again, most had 2 or 3 words after the colon, although 9 of the 57 total had 6 words after the colon. The 2- and 3-word after-the-colon group made up 38 percent of the compound title total. Longest title in this group, a University of Minnesota Press, January 1988, publication: *Understanding Toscanini: How He Became an American Culture-God and Helped Create a New Audience for Old Music.*

Compound titles with 3 words before the colon ranged in overall length from 5 words to 12 words, most having 4, 5, or 6 words after the colon. This grouping represented 25 percent of the total.

Compound titles with 4 words before the colon ranged in overall length from 6 words to 12 words. Surprisingly, for most compound titles that had 4 words before the colon, the number after the colon for 13 of 20 was shorter than the up-front count, usually 1, 2, or 3 words. This group as a whole was 13 percent of the total of all compound titles.

✔ WHEN AND WHEN NOT TO USE HUMOR

Unless the book itself is humorous, humor should be avoided in the title. Editors are uniform in their opinions that a humorous title is otherwise almost always counterproductive.

Although some books on humor identify themselves as such in the title (e.g., *Funniest Joke Book Ever!*) more often than not, the attempt is not *in* the title, but *with* the title, as these examples illustrate:

✦ *You Don't Have to Be Crazy to Work Here. . . But It Sure Helps*

✦ *Guilt Without Sex*

✦ *What's a Nice Girl Like You Doing with a Double Bed?*

✦ *Mercy, It's the Revolution & I'm in My Bathrobe!*

✔ A SAMPLER OF "HOW-TO" TITLES THAT SAY IT SIMPLY AND WELL

◆ *Baby & Child Care*
◆ *Cookin' Cheap*
◆ *How to Be a Better Parent*
◆ *Making Ads Pay*
◆ *Mixing Colors*
◆ *Painting Murals*
◆ *Practical Woodworking*
◆ *Providing for Retirement*
◆ *Publishing Newsletters*
◆ *Starting a Small Restaurant*
◆ *Understanding Photography*
◆ *Writing to Sell*

harmless insignificant and dull

✔ PURPOSELY INNOCUOUS TITLE IS KEY TO BOOK'S SALES SUCCESS: A CASE HISTORY

The book by psychologist Matthew M. Chappell came in to Macmillan Company in the late 1930s bearing the title *Worry and the Peptic Ulcer.*

Howard Cady, then an editorial assistant at Macmillan, liked the book but felt that there might be reluctance on the part of bookstore customers to admit to being worried or to have a book with such a title in their homes. So, with the help of the direct-mail experts at Macmillan, who tested the responses to the original title as compared to a "blue-sky" title, the title was changed to *In the Name of Common Sense.*

During the next three years the book was reprinted again and again. However, after the book had topped 170,000 in sales, the then-president of Macmillan, George T. Brett, Jr., decided it would be better with its original title, *Worry and the Peptic Ulcer.*

As Cady recalls it, direct-mail and bookstore sales of the retitled book came to an abrupt halt. After Macmillan reverted to the less meaningful *In the Name of Common Sense*, the book continued to sell well for many more months.

✓ STILL STUCK FOR A TITLE? SWITCH ON ℰ THE COMPUTER

It is now possible to obtain thought-processor software that will help you with the creation of your book title. *Headliner*™, is a computer library of 25 different databases containing over 33,000 handpicked expressions from hundreds of different sources, including idioms, cliches, puns, song/TV/movie/book titles, quotes, proverbs, and existing slogans.

The *Headliner* computer system runs on a desktop IBM PC or compatible computer and is not "copy protected." The software and databases are on three 5¼" floppy diskettes and come with a user's guide. It is available from The Salinon Corporation, PO Box 31047, Dallas, TX 75231-9990.

"We've had customers use *Headliner* very successfully for book titling," says Mimi Carr of Salinon, "and on August 1, 1987, we dropped the price from $495 to $99."

Some *Headliner* features include:

✦ Key word searching with automatic phrase substitution (search all expressions for a given word).

✦ Rhyme or sound-alike matching (find and display all expressions ending in words that end in "tion," "shun," "done," or "ton").

✦ Acronym/alliteration construction (display all expressions that contain a sequence of words beginning with certain combinations or groups of letters).

CHAPTER 2

BUSINESS AND PROFESSIONAL BOOKS

✓ **TITLING OF PROFESSIONAL BOOKS: OVERALL GUIDELINES***

The title of a book has a commercial significance; it is not simply a matter of personal choice. It is a label. And like any label, it must serve to attract attention, to identify the merchandise, and to distinguish it from other, possibly competing products.

For this reason, publishers often use a tentative, or "working," title until the book has taken final form. They reason that one can name a thing better after it has been written. Because their experience has given them a sense of how the public (and booksellers) might respond, publishers frequently take the lead in nominating a title and recommending it to the author.

A good title for a professional book should be (1) descriptive, (2) specific, (3) distinctive, (4) short, (5) catchy, and (6) easy to remember. Careful reflection on each point is warranted.

1. **Descriptive:** A good title must first describe the contents of the book. The title that describes a work adequately needs no subtitle, jacket blurb, promotional literature, or personal inspection to tell readers that the book deals with a certain aspect of a field that is important to them.

2. **Specific:** A title, to be really useful, should be more than merely descriptive; it should be so specific that prospective readers will know what "slice" of the subject matter the author has carved. The specific title can also distinguish the merits of a book from those of competing works on the same subject. If you believe your book is more useful than an existing work called *Advertising Promotion*, you might consider titling yours *Practical Techniques for Advertising Promotion* to emphasize its concrete, how-to-do-it approach.

---

*Adapted from: *A Practical Guide to Writing and Publishing Professional Books: Business, Technical, Scientific, Scholarly* by Daniel N. Fischel, New York: Van Nostrand Reinhold, 1984. Reprinted with the permission of Daniel N. Fischel.

3. **Distinctive:** A title that meets the tests of being descriptive and specific should also be distinctive. It should have sufficient individuality that it is unlikely to be confused with any similar book. If there already is a *Handbook of Purchasing* and your book is competitive, it would be wise to consider a more distinctive title, such as *Purchasing Manual* or *Manual for Purchasing Managers*.

4. **Short:** The right length for a title is that which conveys the message in the fewest possible words. One word— *Supernovae*—may be enough, particularly if aided by a subtitle. Twelve words may not be too many if circumstances truly warrant, as in *Infrared Systems for Automatic Detection and Tracking of Moving Objects in Space*.

5. **Catchy:** A title should appeal. If possible, it should be catchy. This principle is the one that most frequently must be sacrificed for the sake of the rest, yet if it can be achieved along with the others, it might give your book an appreciable life in the marketplace. *The Meaning of Meaning* is a catchy yet accurate and entirely suitable title for what proved to be a landmark success in the philosophy of communications and semantics.

6. **Easy to Remember:** A title should be easy to remember. It is more likely to be if it is short; avoids unnecessary, difficult, unfamiliar, and polysyllabic words; and avoids odd or awkward constructions. *Lubrication of High-Speed Machinery*, for example, despite the extra word, is smoother than *High-Speed Machinery Lubrication*. Title recall may also be easier if its first word conveys the subject matter. For example, *Welding Manual* comes to mind more readily than *Manual of Welding*. An added benefit is that booklists, card catalogs, and sometimes even booksellers' shelves are often arranged alphabetically, making the title easier to locate.

✔ WHY BUSINESS AND PROFESSIONAL BOOKS NEED STRONG TITLES

A business or professional book has much greater need for a strong, appealing title than a scientific or scholarly book. Here are some reasons why:

1. Such a book must do most of its selling in its first year of life. It often contains information that goes out of date rapidly.

2. Such a book is often a candidate for book clubs; its scientific or scholarly counterparts are not.

3. Such a book has greater chance at impulse buying since it goes into retail bookstores; its scientific and scholarly counterparts do not.
4. A strong title is more likely to appeal to buyers for large bookstore chains.
5. Such a book, as a rule, depends on the domestic market for most of its sales.
6. Such a book title must compete with other trade titles.

TITLES THAT TURN ON BUSINESS MANAGERS

"Business is becoming like engineering," says the marketing manager for business books at a large publishing establishment. "You must master a body of knowledge in order to work. Established managers are realizing they lack the sophistication of younger people just entering the business in such areas as basic computer theory, quantitative techniques in marketing, and more."

This marketing manager says managers will be attracted to book titles that suggest the book's content will keep them current on organizational realities, offer to furnish an understanding of the technical aspects of each new job as they move up the ladder, or promise to increase their knowledge (because they realize that knowledge is power).

TITLES THAT CAPTURE ATTENTION AND IMAGINATION

The title of a business book has to capture both the attention and the imagination of the potential buyer. Business publishers realize they are catering to sophisticated audiences and try to accomplish these two objectives in the title, as the following examples indicate:

✦ *What They Don't Teach You at the Harvard Business School*
✦ *The 50 Plus Guide to Retirement Investing*
✦ *Work Smart, Not Hard*

TURNING A SALES MESSAGE INTO A TITLE

There's no question about it. When you look at the title of the book by CPA Bernard Kamoroff, you have a pretty good idea of what the book is about and what it can do for you: *Small Time Operator:*

How to Start Your Own Small Business, Keep Your Books, Pay Your Taxes and Stay Out of Trouble. At the time of this writing, the book had sold over a quarter of a million copies.

Or consider this title, from Boardroom Books, that has gone through more than a dozen printings: *The Book of Inside Information: Money • Health • Success • Marriage • Education • Car • Collecting • Fitness • Home • Travel • Shopping • Taxes • Investments • Retirement.*

✔ TITLES THAT TALK TO THEIR AUDIENCE

Catherine Rogers, a marketer at Warren, Gorham & Lamont, a New York City-based publisher of business books, offers this view of titling relative to books in accounting, taxation, and finance.

"You have to work closely with your editors and base your title on the book's logical audience so they can relate to it. For example, an accounting book geared to corporate accountants rather than to public accountants should have the word *corporate* in its title so potential buyers will know that the book is aimed at them. A rule we like to follow at Warren, Gorham & Lamont is that the book's title should talk to its audience so that they can identify with it."

✔ KEY WORDS IN BUSINESS BOOKS

According to a study of 260 forthcoming seasonal books from 100 publishers in the fields of business, management, and finance, the word appearing most often in the forthcoming titles, in nearly 9 percent of the total, was *Business*. The second preferred word, appearing in nearly 7 percent of the titles, was *Management*. The third most popular word was one of the forms of *manage—Manage/Managers/Managing*—with over 4 percent. The following list shows the word form and number of appearances in 260 books:

1. *Business*	23	
2. *Management*	18	
3. *Manage/Managers/Managing*	11	
4. *Financial*	10	
5. *Investment/Investor/Investing*	9	
6. *Money*	8	
7. *Entrepreneur/Entrepreneurism/ Entrepreneurial*, tied with *Banks/Banking*	6 each	
8. *Economic/Economics* tied with *Tax*	5 each	
9. *Marketing* tied with *Corporate*	4 each	

10. *Professional/Professionalism* tied with
   boss/bosses and *job*   3 each

A frequently recurring word in the 260 titles was *Guide*, with 22 appearances or approximately 8.5 percent of the total. The most frequent use of *Guide* in a title was as *A Guide to* or *(Publisher Name) Guide to*, appearing 9 times. *A Complete Guide* appeared 3 times, while *Practical Guide* and *Tax Guide to* appeared 2 times each. Other variations of *Guide* included *Pocket Guide, Working Guide, Desktop Guide,* and *Life Guide.*

Handbook appeared in 7 of the 260 titles; *Directory*, 3 times; and *Encyclopedia, Desk Reference,* and *Manual*, once each.

Evidence that business titles frequently serve as their own headlines is evidenced by the fact that 100 of the 260 titles, or over 38 percent, were compound titles separated by a colon.

✓ KEY TITLE WORDS IN BESTSELLING INVESTMENT BOOKS

In the fall of 1987, the key words in 9 of the 10 bestselling investment books in the 950-store Waldenbooks chain (1 of the top 10 was a dictionary) were as follows:

Key Word	Frequency of Use
Guide	5
Understanding	3
Where to/How to	3
You/Your	2
No-Nonsense	2
Investment expert's name	2

✓ KEY WORDS FOR INTERNATIONAL BUSINESS BOOKS

The word *International* is a keyword identifier for books that focus on some aspect of international business, according to a study of new publications listed in *AIB Newsletter*, the quarterly publication of the Academy of International Business. Other key title words in books with international business appeal, though used with considerably less frequency than *International*, are, in descending order, *Foreign, Global, Multinational, Worldwide,* and *Transnational.*

✓ A TITLE THAT MAKES A PROMISE WITH A PROVISO

When a business publisher contracted to publish a small book titled *Risk-Free Advertising*, an alert member of the publisher's marketing staff pointed out that no advertising was entirely risk free and unless modified it was likely to invite buyer complaints.

So a colon was appended to the title and a disclaimer added in a subtitle. Thus, the book was published in 1977 as *Risk-Free Advertising: How to Come Close to It.*

The book enjoyed modest sales success, and there were no reader complaints.

✓ THE PREFERENCE FOR "ING" WORDS IN TITLES

In recent years, various business and professional book publishers have demonstrated a decided preference for starting book titles with gerunds, i.e., words ending in "ing," to give them more action.

There is no common line of reasoning in this popular titling practice. One business book marketer suggested that adding "ing" in business titles conveys an impression that the books will be more helpful to prospective buyers. Currently available business books with "ing" words in their titles include:

- ✦ *Developing New Products*
- ✦ *Franchising Your Business*
- ✦ *Integrating the Computer in Your Business*
- ✦ *Managing by Objectives*
- ✦ *Selling on the Phone*
- ✦ *Starting a Small Restaurant*
- ✦ *Understanding Franchise Contracts*
- ✦ *Winning on Wall Street*

✓ MORE THAN 100 "ING" WORDS TO ADD ACTION TO TITLES

Achieving	Bringing
Acquiring	Building
Advertising	Budgeting
Analyzing	Cashing
Applying	Calculating
Automating	Catching

Changing	Marketing
Checking	Maximizing
Choosing	Merchandising
Climbing	Monitoring
Closing	Negotiating
Communicating	Organizing
Compensating	Originating
Competing	Passing
Conducting	Planning
Contracting	Predicting
Consulting	Preparing
Controlling	Presenting
Coping	Preserving
Counselling	Pricing
Creating	Programming
Designing	Protecting
Developing	Providing
Directing	Publishing
Downsizing	Putting
Eliminating	Rating
Entrepreneuring	Reducing
Evaluating	Reshaping
Expanding	Restoring
Exploring	Revising
Financing	Running
Finding	Scheduling
Forecasting	Selecting
Franchising	Selling
Getting	Solving
Giving	Starting
Going	Staying
Growing	Succeeding
Handling	Supervising
Hedging	Targeting
Implementing	Telling
Improving	Thinking
Increasing	Timing
Integrating	Trading
Initiating	Understanding
Investing	Using
Keeping	Valuing
Launching	Visualizing
Leading	Winning
Making	Working
Managing	Writing

✓ THE IMPORTANCE OF *YOU* IN A NONFICTION TITLE

When Victor O. Schwab, in his classic *How to Write a Good Advertisement* (Harper & Row, 1962), listed 100 winning headlines that had made big money for their users, it turned out that nearly half had the words *You* or *Your* in them.

It should be equally apparent in titling nonfiction books that the words *You* or *Your* can be just as useful in making a title appealing to a potential buyer. Many of the major business book publishers are aware of this factor and try to incorporate *You* or *Your* into their titles, as this title sampling from a single announcement of the American Management Association Book Club indicates:

✦ *How to Save Your Business*

✦ *Manage Your Time, Manage Your Work, Manage Yourself*

✦ *How to Be Your Own Advertising Agency*

✦ *How to Survive and Market Yourself in Management*

✦ *Sacked! What to Do When You Lose Your Job*

✓ PROFESSIONAL TITLE SELLS— SAME BOOK WITH TEXTBOOK TITLE FLOPS—CASE STUDY

In the late 1970s, a business book publisher took a book on a specific aspect of accounting and financial management and issued it simultaneously with different titles and slightly altered contents.

One version was written at an introductory level in collaboration with a professor and issued as a textbook for classroom use. To establish its introductory level, the student-version title led off with *Principles of.* The student version was heavily sampled, but sold relatively few copies beyond the approximately 2,000 given away as complimentary copies.

The professional version, costing nearly 50 percent more, and with the words *Guide to* in the title, sold close to 15,000 copies. It was considered a huge success. The number of review copies, "comps," or other gratis copies did not exceed 1 percent of the total number of copies sold.

A search for answers to the wide disparity in the sales histories of the two differently titled books produced three conclusions:

1. The version with the "professional" title was viewed by working professionals as a reference source on a topic likely to be encountered. They bought it as a working tool.

2. The version with the "textbook" title covered a specialized topic which, while it embraced a specific course, was not perceived by academics as a primary area of concern. Thus, minimal sales.

3. Titling a book as a textbook does not make it a textbook unless there is a perceived legitimate learning need for the topic covered. In this instance, a few professors actually adopted the version of the book with the professional title. Apparently, they felt it enabled their students to grasp the professional aspects of the subject, rather than the basics as presented in the *Principles of* introductory text.

✓ APPENDING ART TO TITLE TO GIVE IT SPECIAL MEANING

Not infrequently in publishing a book title is greatly enhanced by an illustration or symbol that lends credence or understanding to the printed title. One such incident happened in the late 1970s, when a business book publisher was about to launch a book on finance for individuals with little or no knowledge of the subject. The title: *Finance for the Nonfinancial Manager.*

A concern was raised that bookstore browsers and mail order prospects who lacked knowledge of the subject would be turned off by a title that had variations of the word "Finance" twice in the title.

The book's marketing manager posed a solution: do something with the title so it wouldn't make the book look too serious.

The way it was done was to add, directly under the book's title, a large cartoon, taken from *The New Yorker* magazine, of a boardroom scene with a humorous caption.

The combination of title plus cartoon worked, and the book sold into the middle 20,000s and went to a second edition.

"Why it worked," explains the marketer responsible, "is that the combination of title and cartoon tells the prospective buyer what level the book is at and that the reader doesn't have to suffer. The cartoon had become part of the overall title effect."

✓ GUIDELINES FOR TITLE APPEAL IN OVERSEAS MARKETS

For business books to sell well in overseas markets, certain keywords help them find more ready acceptance. These are the seven keywords or phrases found effective by one marketer: *Futures, Commodities, Manufacturing, Strategic Management, International Finance, Forecasting,* and *International Banking.*

Book titles bearing any of these three words generally will not find acceptance in foreign markets: *Small Business, Real Estate,* or *Law.*

In general terms, to do well overseas business titles should stress the practical; offer help in any of the management skills—time management, negotiating, marketing, etc.; or promise concrete assistance in any of the areas that middle-managers face.

Examples of *management skills* titles advertised by Wildwood House, a U.K. business publisher, in the July 3, 1987, issue of *The Bookseller* include: *The Complete Manager, Executive Time Management, Motivational Leadership,* and *Skills of Negotiating.*

CHAPTER 3

SCHOLARLY BOOKS

✓ TITLING ESSENTIALS: A VETERAN MARKETER'S VIEWS

The Scholar's Bookshelf is a Princeton, New Jersey-based mail order operation that offers sharply discounted publishers' overstock titles in the humanities, fine arts, science, and technology to scholars and libraries worldwide.

We talked with Abbott Friedland, its founder and operator and for many years head of marketing for a major university press, about titles and their influence on his book selections.

Says Friedland: "If I see an interesting-sounding title, I tend to give it more consideration. Titles are extremely important in the mail order catalog business, where you must include a large number of titles and give each very short annotations.

"We particularly like books that have a good title and subtitle because, as a rule, we can use a title listing as the complete entry. On the other hand, there are a great many book titles that say nothing.

"In my business, if the title does not describe the book it puts us at a great disadvantage. For many publishers, there seems to be a tendency to go in two directions, especially in literary criticism or history. Often an author wants a title that might be more appropriate for a work of fiction—one that has nothing to do with the content of the book. That type of title I find to be totally unusable, and, I might add, as a rule unsuccessful.

"The other extreme is the title that describes a book, but not in a positive sense. What I mean is that the title underplays the true importance of the book, and the book is much more important than its title implies.

"Many a scholarly title is often to the left or right of the true coverage of the book and covers only a small part of what the book is really about. When we run into such a book, that is, one whose title doesn't give its importance to its main audience, we have to try to make up for the title's shortcoming by providing a more detailed description in the copy following.

"Titles that don't convey a book's full meaning may be all right for books that get popular media attention, where enough advertising and exploitation will get across the book's full store. But this is generally not the case for books directed to specialized audiences.

"If a reader is buying a book for its content and the title has nothing to do with the content or the book's subject, the book is likely to be a failure.

"The ideal is a book title that gets right into the center of the book's subject and presents its main appeal to the widest possible number of prospective readers."

✓ RIGHT AND WRONG TITLES: VIEWS FROM AN EXPERT

This contribution on book titling is of special interest, since its author wears many hats involving book titles. He is Irving Louis Horowitz of Rutgers University. Horowitz is both president of Transaction Books and editor-in-chief of *Society* magazine, a publication serving the social sciences. He is also review editor of *Society* and author or contributor to scores of books in the social sciences.

Says Horowitz: "Since titling is a subject of vast proportions, I'll confine myself to a single point, one that has been and remains a touchstone for the way Transaction Publishers and *Society* magazine alike operate.

"Whether considering a book for publication or for review purposes in the magazine, I look for an isomorphism between the contents of the book and its title.

"In scholarly and scientific communication, what is crucial is precision, not abstract 'catchy' titles. If a book is on mining and ranching in North Dakota it should be so called, not something like *Treasures and Romances of the Plains*. If a book is on ruling elites and policy making it should be so called, not something like *High Society*.

"In principle, a title is wrong when any of a bakers dozen can go by the same phrases. A title is right when it defines and delineates its contents. The reader (who is the buyer) deserves the truth in packaging. Hype is dangerous, inviting the Lincolnesque retort of not fooling all the people all of the time. Indeed, good titles will suggest themselves from good manuscripts. At least that has been my experience."

✓ PUBLISHING SOURCE AS KEY TO CREDIBILITY

Many scholarly authors favor having their works published by university presses. They are convinced that scholarly titles gain credibility from a university press and that a "name" university press will lend more credibility to their title than a commercial house, largely because university press titles are approved for publication by a committee of faculty members who assess, screen, and select only the most worthy submissions.

Here are some supporting arguments for this theory:

✦ University presses usually publish specialized scholarly books for well-defined markets and are able to reach these markets.

✦ University presses enjoy a large measure of imprint loyalty. Their customers are familiar with the publisher's imprint and look for other books from that press.

✦ A title issued by a university press often encounters less price resistance than one issued by a commercial counterpart.

✦ A title by a little-known author can be greatly enhanced by the prestige of the issuing press, such as an engineering treatise by a young unknown issued by MIT Press.

✓ CONCERNS FROM AN ACADEMIC COLLECTION DEVELOPMENT LIBRARIAN

"A book title," says Dora Biblarz, "should have words in it that tell what the book is about. This is not only helpful to me as a collection development librarian, but also to the students who use the library here at Arizona State University.

"Some publishers," adds Ms. Biblarz, "may have a different perspective about book titles. They want a title to be memorable. But it sometimes creates problems with readers who have difficulty remembering a title if it doesn't identify the book.

"My pet peeve in book titling is the book that promises a lot in the title and then doesn't deliver. What I expect in a good title is one that will tell me, as closely as possible, what I can expect in the contents—particularly as it relates to scholarly books.

"For major reference works, like encyclopedias and dictionaries, I will often opt for a book with a questionable title if I respect the authority of the publisher. For example, if the book was from Encyclopaedia Britannica, I wouldn't hesitate to order it, and to trust its contents. We don't always know the authors of forthcoming books, but if the book is from a good house, I'd be inclined to take a chance on it, based on the publisher's reputation."

✓ SCHOLARLY BOOK TITLE APPEALS FOR ACADEMIC LIBRARIES

The heaviest buyers of scholarly books are academic libraries. As a rule, book purchases are related to the school curriculum. Therefore, subject and level of a particular book are of crucial importance if it is possible to incorporate these factors into a book title.

Highly specialized books are often bought on the strength of their titles alone, as is evidenced in this remark by a university acquisitions librarian in a presentation at a meeting of university presses in 1975:

> Take a book on Pomeranian swine exports. . . . Any scholar who is going to buy the book, or ask the library to buy it, is already going to be crazy about Pomeranian swine. [He] does not need a copywriter to tell him about it at great length, [but] some indication of the author's qualifications carries great weight.

✓ BOOK TITLES AS BUYING TURN-OFF: VIEWS FROM A SCHOLARLY LIBRARY SUPPLIER

"Titles are important only to the degree that they indicate topicality." The speaker is Helmut Schwartzer, a veteran bookbuyer for a New England-based supplier of books to academic and scholarly libraries.

Schwartzer continues, "Titles do influence us [jobbers] in a negative way, however. They are able to tell us that the books do not qualify for our market. We look at a title and dismiss it immediately if it is apparent to us that it is not in one of the areas of our concern."

Schwartzer also made this observation about a trend he has seen in recent years in academic/scholarly book titling: "One thing that has become popular with so many titles for the academic/scholarly market is that the key information we seek about a book has often been relegated to the subtitle. . . . We have learned to read subtitles to learn about the appropriateness of books for our needs.

"Insofar as the value of titles as selling tools in and of themselves, we base our promotion of books to our [library] markets on examination of the book in hand—by perusing the contents. We are not influenced solely by the title of the book for our market."

✓ WHY YOU SHOULD INCORPORATE "SELL" INTO SCHOLARLY TITLES

Many professional and scholarly periodicals, which may not carry a review of a submitted review book for years, if ever, will however often provide a complete bibliographic description of all new books received for review, usually under a heading such as "New Books" or "Books Received."*

The subscribers to these publications often make it a practice to review these "New Books" listings to ascertain the new publications in their fields and will often order for examination or recommend acquisition solely on the basis of the title appeal.

Consequently, the more precisely the title portrays the book, the more likely it is to be ordered or recommended by the professional having need for or interest in such information.

✔ THE BINARY TITLE

A category of book title that has prevailed in intellectual works for centuries is the binary, or two-part, title. In such titles, two unrelated words, usually impressive and often similar sounding, are joined together to form a book title (e.g., *Conjunctions and Disjunctions*).

A detailed examination of the binary title is made by Herbert McArthur, research scholar at State University of New York, in *Scholarly Publishing*.† In it, he says the rhetorical message of such a title is an imposing one for any type of intellectual work because the device implies two large and weighty concepts are brought together, a more wondrous feat than the essay of one topic.

MacArthur's article includes a substantial sampling of some of the better literary works of this century that have followed this formula, a small sample of which are:

- ✦ *Rousseau and Romanticism* (Babbitt, 1919)
- ✦ *Mysticism and Logic* (Bertrand Russell, 1925)
- ✦ *Education and the Good Life* (Russell, 1926)
- ✦ *Being and Time* (Heidegger, 1927)
- ✦ *Ideology and Utopia* (Mannheim, 1929)
- ✦ *Marriage and Morals* (Russell, 1929)
- ✦ *Poetry and Mathematics* (Buchanan, 1929)
- ✦ *Progress and Power* (Becker, 1936)
- ✦ *Being and Nothingness* (Sartre, 1943)
- ✦ *Science and Criticism* (Muller, 1943)

Science, a weekly journal for the American scientific community with a subscriber base of over 156,000, carries a "Books Received" section in each issue for all new books received for review. Subsequently, only about 1 in every 15 books listed will receive a full-length review. Source: *Book Marketing Handbook*, Vol. 2, by Nat Bodian. New York: R.R. Bowker, 1984.

†In "Tomes and Titles," *Scholarly Publishing* 12 (no. 2): January 1981.

✦ *Image and Idea* (Rahv, 1949)
✦ *Childhood and Society* (Erikson, 1950)
✦ *Genesis and Geology* (Gillispie, 1951)
✦ *Paradox and Nirvana* (Slater, 1951)
✦ *Feeling and Form* (Langer, 1953)
✦ *Eros and Civilization* (Marcuse, 1955)
✦ *Language and Logic* (Russell, 1956)
✦ *Science and Imagination* (Nicolson, 1956)
✦ *Art and Psychoanalysis* (Phillips, 1957)
✦ *Ancients and Moderns* (Jones, 1961)
✦ *Psychoanalysis and History* (Mazlish, 1963)
✦ *Language and Mind* (Chomsky, 1968)
✦ *Tragedy and Philosophy* (Kaufmann, 1968)
✦ *Art and Pornography* (Peckham, 1969)
✦ *Knowledge and Freedom* (Russell, 1971)
✦ *Entropy and Art* (Arnheim, 1971)
✦ *Vision and Resonance* (Hollander, 1975)
✦ *Liberty and Language* (Geoffrey Sampson, 1979)

✓ THE CROWDED CROSSROADS

A title form popular over the years is one at the "crossroads" of something, as the following brief sampling indicates.

Be warned, however, that if you start your title with *Crossroads*, you're going to have a lot of company in the abstracting and indexing services and in *Books in Print*.

✦ *Engineering Education at the Crossroads* (Asch)
✦ *Crossroads to the Cinema* (Brode)
✦ *Crossroads in Philosophy: Existentialism, Naturalism, Theistic Realism* (Collins)
✦ *Crossroads in Korea* (Fehrenbach)
✦ *Crossroads of Liberalism: Croly, Weyl, Lippman, and The Progressive Era* (Forcey)
✦ *Crossroads: Proceedings of the First National Conference of the Library and Information Technology Association* (Gorman)
✦ *Crossroads of Civilization: Three Thousand Years of Persian History* (Irving)
✦ *Crossroads of Decision: The State Department and Foreign Policy* (Jablon)

✦ *Crossroads: Quality of Life Through Rhetorical Modes* (Kakonis)
✦ *Crossroads: A Back to School Career Guide for Adults* (Moore)
✦ *Crossroads of Power* (Namier)
✦ *Crossroads in Cooking* (Pappas)
✦ *Crossroads: Essayists on the Catholic Novelists* (Sonnelfeld)
✦ *Private Black Colleges at the Crossroads* (Thompson)

✓ TITLING THE *FESTSCHRIFT*, OR HOMAGE VOLUME

A highly specialized type of scholarly publication is the homage volume, or *Festschrift*. Consisting of essays by former students, it generally honors a retiring scholar or commemorates a highly regarded one on some special occasion, such as a particular birthday.

Festschrift titles are usually compound, with a colon, and refer to the honoree in the second part. A few examples:

✦ *Immigration and American History: Essays in Honor of Theodore Blegan*
✦ *In the Trek of the Immigrants: Essays Presented to Carl White*
✦ *Essays on the American Constitution: A Commemorative Volume in Honor of Alpheus T. Mason*

✓ LAW BOOKS: LAW LIBRARIANS LOOK FOR CURRENTNESS AND CREDENTIALS

Customarily, law librarians buy a book on the basis of the subject and the currentness of the material. They also favor a book by an author with strong legal credentials in the subject area of the book or from a publisher with a track record for high-quality law books.

Since the title carries a large portion of the selling burden, it must accurately portray the subject and how the book addresses it.

CHAPTER 4

NEW EDITIONS, SERIES, SERIALS, AND SETS

✔ TITLING SERIALS, SERIES, AND SETS: ADVICE FROM A LIBRARY AUTHORITY

The comments following on titling of serials, series, and sets are a contribution of Marcia Romanansky, a longtime library professional, who is currently marketing director for public libraries at Baker & Taylor, America's oldest and largest wholesale bookseller. Her career as a library professional also included five years at the library of St. Peters College in Jersey City, New Jersey.

On Serials: "If you're titling a serial (like *World Almanac* or equivalent), always put the main title up front, with the date following. If you don't, you create a problem for the librarian. And be sure to keep the serial title standard for the life of the serial."

On Series: "If you're tying together essentially independent books with a series name (e.g., *Computer Desk Reference: Lotus 1-2-3*) and you will be having other books also starting with "Computer Desk Reference," it's a good idea to make the "Lotus 1-2-3" the main title and use the series name (e.g., *Computer Desk Reference*) as the subtitle. You need to establish such books by their titles, rather than by the series name."

On Sets: "If you have a set such as *The Papers of George Washington*, Volume 5: *The Revolutionary Years*, bear in mind that sets go by the name of the set. It should be clear that a set holds its name for all the volumes. Each book is part of that set, even if it can be purchased alone. In sets, the common thread between all volumes should be the set name. You should always think of any one book in a set, as in the "Washington" example above, as Volume 5 of *The Papers of George Washington*."

✔ SHOULD A BOOK HAVE A SERIES LABEL AS WELL AS TITLE?—PROS AND CONS

Series are a way of life in scientific and scholarly publishing. Adding a series "label" to a book's title ensures not only ready-made recognition for newly published books but also faster acceptance of previously unpublished or little-known authors.

Further, tying a book's title to a series will often ensure a longer life for a published work than it might enjoy as an independent book.

Series should not be confused with *serials*. The *series* book is part of a collection in a single subject area. The *serial* book is a publication issued in successive parts, usually bearing numerical or chronological designations and intended to be continued indefinitely. (A broader definition of *serials* would also include periodicals, newspapers, annuals, proceedings, and transactions of societies, and numbered monographic series.)

A *series* consists of volumes, each a complete segment of the series subject area. A *serial* usually has one editor (or grouping of editors), and each volume consists of a collection of chapters, unrelated to each other, but each being a subset of the overall subject area of the serial. It is not unusual for a chapter in a *serial* to be expanded into a volume in a *series*.

Scientific and technical series in some specialized areas may be published in uniform sizes, with similar bindings and jacket designs. This would be true of most series by the same author or same editor. In such series, new volumes require only slight modification in binding and jacket design—the design being a contributing factor in series recognition.

A series can be created for any group of books that serve an interest group, a discipline, or any sub-branch of one. Unless it is a standardized series, such as the parts of an encyclopedia published over successive periods, books in a series may be in identical or different formats. Sometimes individual volumes in a series carry the series identification only on the jacket—sometimes, not at all.

An example of a longtime successful series in nonstandardized format is the Wiley Series in Probability and Mathematical Statistics. This series encompasses virtually all of the publisher's professional titles within the subject area. There are close to 200 titles under this series heading. In this example, the series name serves to identify the publisher as one of the leaders in this area of publishing and the book as appropriate for the practicing professional. Each title within this Wiley series is treated as an individual new work and marketed on its own merits. There is virtually no carryover from one series title to another, but being part of the series does aid in the book's recognition and, therefore, its sales.

Series sell better to libraries. Often, when a library considers a series important to its collection, it will place a standing order for the entire series, i.e., automatically buy new volumes as they are published. Thus one benefit of a series is a virtually automatic sale to libraries with little more promotion than that the next book in the series is available.

Are there any disadvantages to a book being in a series? Yes, say some marketers who feel there is a certain amount of risk in a book achieving its true potential because it is "buried" in a series. Because the series has its own built-in sales momentum, some series titles might not get the promotional push they might have if announced and promoted on their own.

How do authors view series? Most authors have no apprehensions about having their work as part of a series, especially if it is a prestigious one within its field. Lesser-known authors may favor having their work tied into an established series because it offers an opportunity to soak up some of the prestige of the overall series—prestige that their published work most likely would not attain if published in the author's name alone.

A well-known author or acknowledged leader in the field, on the other hand, might be reluctant to submerge his or her own individuality by having his or her work as part of a series unless other "name" authors are also part of the same series.

✓ CHANGING A SERIAL TITLE TO IMPROVE MARKETABILITY

You've launched the first volume of a new annual, and it fails to take off. The content of the initial offering is excellent, but its title is uninspired. You decide that an improved title might improve marketability.

Your original title was something like "Publix Press Yearbook." Let us assume your press has a good list in toxicology research and a reputation as a publisher in that field. Possibly your yearbook is a collection of the best toxicological research of the preceding year.

How best to go about the title change?

One alternative, having already launched the serial, is to change the title while not necessarily discarding the existing title. Here are some suggested ways of doing this:

ALTERNATIVE 1

(in small type on one line)   Publix Press Yearbook
of

(in larger display type, the new title)   TOXICOLOGY
RESEARCH
1989

ALTERNATIVE 2

(in larger display type)   TOXICOLOGY
RESEARCH
1989

(and in small type, the former title on one
line)   formerly Publix Press
Yearbook

ALTERNATIVE 3

(in larger display type, the new title)   TOXICOLOGY
RESEARCH
1989

(and in smaller type, add the former title as
subtitle)   A Publix Press
Yearbook

✓ TITLING: FOR STATE-OF-THE-ART SERIES WITH "ADVANCES" OR "PROGRESS" TITLES

There are series with state-of-the-art information on a particular subject, usually in the sciences. Titling is simple: it is the name of the subject covered. Such works usually contain three to eight chapters and may be issued as often as a couple of times a year or as infrequently as one volume every two or three years.

Occasionally, when such a series includes a topical volume—i.e., one in which all the contributions are on a specific topic within the subject area—it is a good idea to include prominently the title of the topic on the jacket or cover along with the series title and volume number.

Experience has shown that titled (topical) volumes in such series tend to outsell volumes that carry only the series name and volume number.

In some instances, when the topic is deemed important enough, a publisher may depart from the usually drab series jacket or cover and provide the volume with a special display jacket so that the book can be promoted independently for additional sales beyond those to series buyers or subscribers. In such efforts, the title is prominent and the series name either omitted on the jacket or considerably played down, giving the book the appearance of being an independent work.

Some typical series titles with "Advances" or "Progress" are:

✦ Advances in Chemical Physics
✦ Advances in Enzymology
✦ Progress in Inorganic Chemistry
✦ Progress in Macrocyclic Chemistry

✔ SERIES TITLING WHEN EACH VOLUME STANDS ALONE

There is a type of series in scientific publishing that starts with "A Treatise on..." or "Techniques of..." or "Compendium of..." or the like, in which the individual volumes in the series stand alone.

Normally each volume is devoted to complete up-to-date coverage of a single topic or group of related topics. The content is intended to be timeless. Although part of the series, the individual volumes usually succeed or fail on the merits of the individual titles. However, many libraries enter subscriptions for the series and will buy each volume as part of their series subscription.

Typical volumes in such a series will have this information as title:

✦ *Treatise on Analytical Chemistry, Volume 14: Theory and Practice*
✦ *Techniques of Chemistry, Volume 9: Chemical Experimentation Under Extreme Conditions*

✔ AN UNORTHODOX APPROACH TO SERIES TITLING

Typically, publishers create a series title and then create or locate titles to fit the series heading. However, one publisher in the 1960s created a series in which the name of the series was fitted into each title, a formula now in wide use.

The series was a set of specialized dictionaries on various scientific disciplines—mathematics, chemistry, physics, etc.

The master title created for *all* the series volumes was *Dictionary of* _____ : *Abbreviations, Signs, and Symbols.*

Then as each title was prepared, the appropriate subject word was inserted to complete the title, for example: *Dictionary of Chemistry: Abbreviations, Signs, and Symbols.*

✔ *REVISED EDITION* OR *UPDATED EDITION* IN TITLE: WHEN TO USE EACH

When a published work is reissued in changed form, the title may often include the words *Revised Edition* or *Updated Edition.* When is each usage appropriate?

✦ *Revised Edition*—Use when there has been a complete reexamination of the previous edition, where the work has sufficient changes or new material to enable it to be offered as a new work, and where it has been completely retypeset.

✦ *Updated Edition*—Use when there has been a correction of errors and where there has been a substitution of new material for old material, but not a complete resetting of the original text.

✔ TITLE CHANGE REVERSES SECOND EDITION FALLOFF: A CASE STUDY

Second editions of professional and reference books, unlike successful textbooks, tend to have a falloff in sales from the original work.

Sometimes it is possible, through a slight change of title, to reverse this process. A good example of how this principle is put into practice may be seen in the case of a reference book by Victor Showers, originally published by Wiley in 1973.

When Wiley contracted to issue a second edition in 1979, it came under my responsibility as marketing manager of the Interscience Division. Aware of the trend toward second edition sales falloff and aware that this book was essentially a book of "facts," I suggested a title change from *World in Figures* to *World Facts and Figures.*

World Facts and Figures, published in 1979, sold over 40 percent more copies than its original counterpart, *World in Figures.*

✔ HOW TO CREATE, TITLE, AND SELL OLDER BOOKS IN SETS AS NEW PRODUCTS

Here is a form of book titling that I have practiced for many years with great success: the creation of sets. It works well with published collections of research or information in the sciences.

A set usually consists of a group of books published and sold individually over a period of years, most usually as part of a named series or as numbered volumes published sequentially.

Creating the set consists of assembling all the volumes published to date, grouping them into a single entity with its own title and order number, and offering this group as a new product at a special "set price."

Such groupings tend to provide the publisher with a source of "plus sales" and can be advertised and promoted at relatively no cost when tied to the promotional efforts of the newest volume in the grouping. The publisher in effect has two new products and, at the same time, gives new life to the older, slow-moving titles in the group.

A variant of set creation is to pull together independent titles (by the same or different authors) with a sufficiently strong common theme and re-create them as a set.

If you are in a position to consider the creation of sets, titling should not pose a problem. Here are some tested and proven guidelines to follow:

If the assembled volumes are numbered volumes in a series, for example, and the series name is Medical Computing, titling is simple. Say you've just issued Volume 5. You offer Volume 5 as a single new volume and, along with it, you offer your newly created five-volume set, consisting of all volumes published to date. You title the set *Medical Computing, 5-Volume Set* (and you price the set at a small saving off the collective single-volume prices).

Should you subsequently issue a Volume 6 of *Medical Computing*, then you place the five-volume set out of print and create a new set titled *Medical Computing, 6-Volume Set*.

If you decided to create sets from your book products, there are four rules to bear in mind that will enable you to implement the practice without problems:

1. Each set created gets its own ISBN (International Standard Book Number) for ease of identification and tracking.
2. Each set must be given its own unique title.
3. Each set must be given its own "set description" in the publisher's catalog or in advertising, although this is usually

not necessary when the set is appended to promotion of the most recent volume or title.

4. Because the dates of the set volumes span a number of years, do not show as publication date the year the set was created (this tends to confuse librarians who may have already purchased the earlier volumes in the set). Instead show the years of the oldest and newest volumes. If the first volume was published in 1981, and the fifth volume in 1989, show the publication date for the five-volume set as 1981/1989.

If, on the other hand, you have selected compatible titles not part of a common-name series, strive for a title that strikes a common ground. Here is an example of a set I created by joining two compatible titles by the same author but not part of a series:

✦ First title: *Theory of Point Estimation*
✦ Second title: *Testing Statistical Hypotheses*
✦ Set title: *Testing and Estimation in Statistics*

How to handle the catalog description of unrelated but compatible titles? Below is the catalog description I wrote for this set:

Two works covering various aspects of statistical inference. The second edition of *Testing Statistical Hypotheses* is devoted entirely to the theory of hypothesis testing and of estimation by confidence intervals. The companion volume, *Theory of Point Estimation*, provides a comprehensive account in Euclidean sample spaces, and includes nearly 700 problems of theory and applications.

✔ WHEN THE SET OFFERING IS A MIXED BAG: GUIDELINE FOR TITLING

Still one other form of set occasionally offered by publishers is a set composed of an unrelated and not-compatible grouping of books. A publisher might, for example, offer all of the books within a specific subject or interest area at a single collective price.

Another publisher with a modest seasonal list may offer all of the books listed in the seasonal catalog at a single package price. For such nonrelated groupings, the usual titling approach is to tag the collection a "Library."

The typical title for the unrelated grouping would then take on the publisher's name with "Library" to make the title "The (publisher name) Library." If the seasonal catalog is in a particular subject, such as chemistry, and the offering is for all the books in the catalog, a typical title might be "The (publisher name) Chemistry Library."

CHAPTER 5

TEXTBOOKS

✓ SHOULD THE TITLE APPEAL TO STUDENTS OR TEACHERS?

"Textbooks are written for teachers, not for students," says Rudolph Flesch in *The Art of Plain Talk* (Harper & Row, 1946). And what holds for the book itself holds equally—or even more strongly—for titles. "And what teachers seek in a text," says Flesch, "is something that will be a help in teaching—a labor-saving device."

If your text is indeed a labor-saving device, letting prospective adopters know this up front, preferably in the title, is a good idea.

✓ COLLEGE TEXTBOOK TITLING: SOME THOUGHTS FROM A VETERAN EDITOR

"College textbook titles," says Richard Leyh, a veteran college editor, "are very course driven. For a textbook to be effective, you should be able to look at the book's title and know exactly what course it is for. Here is a good example: *The Shaping of Our World: A Human and Cultural Geography.*

"In the area of language texts, authors often try to be creative rather than descriptive with their titles. The end result, sometimes, is that the title winds up not meaning anything, or else it may tend to mislead its potential audience. *German for Everybody* is a title of a fine text, but what can you get from it?

"By contrast, let me show you a title I call perfect, since it not only points out its subject, but also its niche within that subject: *Discovering Astronomy.* This text title is good because it exemplifies 'approach.' The book really is a hands-on approach to the subject, complete with a kit that includes exercises and instructions on how to build your own telescope. If the book didn't have that hands-on approach, people would really be upset with it, but the title works because it lives up to its promise.

"Not all authors give really serious thought to the titles of their books; when they do, the results can be really satisfying and indicative of the author's knowledge of what the field considers important. Here is another example of textbook titling in which the author not only gave his title serious thought, but took a stand on it and couldn't be swayed.

"The book was a 'principles of management' text and the author had titled it *Management for Productivity*. People here—both in editorial and marketing—warned against the title, said it wasn't clear enough, and urged for a change in title.

"But the author insisted on his choice, *Management for Productivity*, and he was right. The book sold more copies than any introductory text we'd done before in the same area. The author's title was indicative of the book's approach and his conviction that 'the bottomline of management is productivity' and this was what he had incorporated in his title."

✓ WHY THE AUTHOR'S NAME FREQUENTLY OUTWEIGHS THE TITLE IN TEXTBOOKS

Educational publishing is one area where the author's name is more important than the title of the book. For most undergraduate texts, book recommenders, booksellers, and students refer to a particular book by the author's name rather than by the book's title—simply because in virtually any area of instruction, the book is likely to be the name of the course and there may therefore be scores of books bearing the same course name.

This phenomenon should be taken into account in the design of undergraduate textbooks; the author's name should always be clearly distinguishable both on cover or jacket and on the spine.

✓ HOW TO RETAIN COURSE NAME IDENTITY AND STRESS UNIQUE SELLING PROPOSITION

"At the higher (college) level of textbook publishing," says one senior editor, "you have to count on single-copy sales as well as on course adoptions. Having the same title can be detrimental to single-copy sales. With upper-level texts, you have to be more careful in titling."

A useful approach to titling books in the same subject areas is to adopt a compound title with the same-name title to the left of the colon and the uniqueness of the particular title or its main thrust to the right in the form of a subtitle. Seek out what is known in advertising as the USP (unique selling proposition).

Some examples of this are:

✦ *Analytical Chemistry: An Introduction Emphasizing Statistical Approaches*

✦ *Population Ecology: An Evolutionary Approach*

✦ *Designing Digital Filters: A Nonmathematical Approach*

✦ *Soil Physics: A Text Emphasizing the Arrangement of Soil Solids*

✔ TEXTBOOK TITLES THAT IMPLY COURSE NAME WITHOUT USING IT

In the social sciences, it is often possible to get away from a course name in a book title by using a title that incorporates words that tell a potential adopter for which course a book is designed.

Gary Belkin, in *Getting Published* (Wiley, 1984), cites these examples of titles with wording that clearly indicates the course for which it is intended:

Title	Name of Course Intended for
Understanding People	Introduction to Psychology
Civilization in Progress	World History
The Helping Relationship	Counseling/Psychotherapy

✔ TITLING A GRADUATE-LEVEL TEXT: TWO EXPERTS CONCUR

"A graduate level text," says Herb Reich, a seasoned social science editor, "has to bear the cachet of being an advanced work. It has to avoid such words as *Basics of* or *Introduction to*. Its tone must give the reader a certain position or status on the educational ladder past the introductory."

Professor Cecil Reynolds, coauthor of the two top-selling textbooks in the field of school psychology, concurs about avoiding the word "Introduction" in a title, adding that "graduate schools frown on *Introduction* or *Introductory* in a title."

CHAPTER 6

DICTIONARIES

✔ THE POWER OF *DICTIONARY* AS WORD IN TITLE

"Dictionary," says Sidney Landau, editor-in-chief at Funk & Wagnalls dictionaries for seven years and involved in dictionaries for more than 25 years, "is a powerful word. Authors and publishers have found that if they call a reference book a *Dictionary* it tends to sell better than it would if called by another name because the word suggests authority, scholarship, and precision.

"As an author," Landau says, "when you have produced a dictionary, you have produced a work of enduring value, and usually one of much greater longevity than other types of references."

The selling power of the word "Dictionary" is thrown into sharp relief by an incident involving the chief executive of the American affiliate of a European scientific publisher. Visiting the parent company, he came upon a vaguely titled physics manuscript about to go into production. He fanned the manuscript pages and found it to be a book with an alphabetical arrangement of words and their definitions.

"This," he said, "is a dictionary. If you expect me to sell it in the United States, the title had better call the book what it is—a dictionary."

The book was retitled *Dictionary of (its original title in physics)*. A simple change of title had most likely saved the book from what might well have been oblivion.

✔ WHEN TO USE *DICTIONARY* AND WHEN TO USE *ENCYCLOPEDIA* IN A TITLE*

Dictionary definitions are usually confined to information that the reader must have to understand an unfamiliar word. The emphasis is on the word, and the information bears directly on its meaning, pronunciation, use, or history.

Encyclopedia articles are essentially topical, dealing with the entire subject represented by the article's title. An encyclopedia article

---

*Adapted from: *Dictionaries: The Art and Craft of Lexicography* by Sidney I. Landau, New York: Charles Scribner's Sons, 1984. Used with the permission of the author.

on religion does not merely say what the word "religion" means or has meant in the past or how it is pronounced or used. It systematically describes the religions of the world.

Simply stated, if your book is about *words*, call it a *dictionary*. If it is about *things*, call it an *encyclopedia*.

✓ TITLING PATTERNS, KEY WORDS, AND SUBJECT COVERAGE

Specialized dictionaries represent a good growth area in reference and scholarly publishing. The book selection magazine *Choice*, published by the Association of College and Research Libraries, reviews a range of titles that are deemed appropriate for librarians, faculty, students, scholars, and the informed public, and are suited for undergraduate college library collections.

Of the nearly 6,000 titles selected for review during the publication year ending August 1987, approximately 45 were dictionaries. Here is what a study of these dictionary titles indicated:

✦ 30 started with *Dictionary of.*

✦ 1 each started with *Concise Dictionary of, Encyclopedic Dictionary of, Historic Dictionary of, International Dictionary of.*

✦ 3 started with *New Dictionary of.*

✦ 6 started with the subject of the dictionary up front, ahead of the word *Dictionary.*

✦ 1 used the word *Glossary* in the title instead of *Dictionary.*

Several more dictionaries started with a name up front identified either with the compiler or with the publisher (e.g., *Facts on File Dictionary of Nonprofit Organizations*).

Subjects covered ranged from American slang to Albanian literature, from Chinese symbols to Christian theology, from military terms to pharmacy, from semiotics and sports to toponyms.

✓ MOST POPULAR TITLE STARTERS

By far the overwhelming titling choice of all dictionary names in print are those that start with *Dictionary of*—approximately 1,400.

But there are numerous other dictionaries that take their names from their newness or type of format. After *Dictionary of*, the most frequent name choice for dictionaries is *Concise Dictionary of* (42), closely followed by *Illustrated Dictionary of* (39).

In fourth place are works starting with *New Dictionary of* (20), followed by *Comprehensive Dictionary of* (18). Surprisingly, the 1987-88 edition of *Books in Print* lists only one *Comprehensive Dictionary of.*

✓ DICTIONARY-TITLED WORKS VOTED MOST USEFUL REFERENCES*

When the Columbia University Graduate School of Journalism polled its students on the reference works they had found most useful, 9 in the top 20 included the word "Dictionary" in the title. The next closest contender was "Encyclopedia", with 2. Among the remaining 9 were such singles as "Almanac," "Atlas," "Bible," "Quotations," and "Thesaurus."

✓ WHY, WHEN, AND HOW SOME BOOKS AVOID *DICTIONARY* IN THE TITLE

According to the *Random House Dictionary of the English Language,* 1966 edition, one definition of a dictionary is "a book giving information on a particular subject or on a particular class of words, names, or facts usually arranged alphabetically."

However, many books in dictionary format avoid using the word "Dictionary" in the title.

There are probably many reasons for this avoidance, one of which may be an effort to be "cute" or "creative."† However, most of the time it is for one of these reasons:

1. The author feels the book is more than just a dictionary.
2. The level of presentation is for very young readers, and a less intimidating word than "Dictionary" is preferred.
3. A less formal appearance than that of a dictionary is desired.
4. The author feels the subject matter is more important than the format and does not want the work to be thought of as a dictionary.
5. The author wants to make the title seem more potent than is indicated by the word "Dictionary," as in the case of the

---

Book of Inside Information edited by Bottom Line Personal Experts, New York: Boardroom Books, 1986.

†A dictionary satire of "imagined origins for 300 figures of speech," published January 1988 by Fawcett Columbine, New York, bore the unlikely title: *The Cat's Pajamas: A Fabulous Fictionary of Familiar Phrases.*

work titled *Handbook of Terms Used in Algebra and Analysis*.

✓ RETAINING MAIN TITLE ON DICTIONARY SPINOFFS

When you have a title that has had time to saturate its primary markets, but may not have reached its peripheral markets, either because of size or price, you can still capitalize on the name and fame of your main title by creating spinoffs that retain the name.

W. & R. Chambers, publisher of the impressive *Chambers 20th Century Dictionary*, clearly demonstrated this in 1987 when it simultaneously spun off three scaled-down versions of its larger work, all retaining the "Chambers" name and two of them also the "20th Century" name. All of the 1987 publications were derived from the main work, which has 176,000 references and a quarter million definitions and sells in hardcover for $24.95.

The first spinoff title was *Chambers Concise 20th Century Dictionary*, a hardcover work about one-half the size of the larger work, priced at $15.95.

The second spinoff was *Chambers Pocket 20th Century Dictionary*, about one-fifth the size of the main work and priced at $6.95 in hardcover.

The third spinoff was *Chambers Mini-Dictionary*, a $3.95 paperback about one-seventh the size of the main work.

✓ COMICAL WEBSTER'S USES TITLE AS SAMPLE OF CONTENT: CASE STUDY

From the field of women's studies comes the most unusual version of a "Webster" dictionary yet conceived. Published by Beacon Press in late 1987, it was the creation of feminist Mary Daly. The title is *Webster's First New Intergalactic Wickedary of the English Language*. The publisher's catalog describes it as "the Labyrinthine Journey of the *Wickedary*—a Wicked, Wiccen dictionary for Witches—moves through three phases (representing front matter, word definitions, and essays)."

Author Mary Daly is described in the catalog as "a Positively Revolting Hag who teaches feminist ethics in the Department of Theology at Boston College."

✓ *WEBSTER* AND *ROGET* MOST WIDELY USED DICTIONARY NAMES

Considering a dictionary or thesaurus? If you are, you can join the growing list of those who include *Webster* or *Roget* in their titles. Both of these names, based on early 19th-century classics, have fallen into the public domain and may now be used by anyone doing a compilation that falls into either format.

Bear in mind, however, that there are more than 40 publications currently in print that include in their titles the words *Webster's Dictionary* and more than 10 that include *Roget's Thesaurus*; any late "me-to" effort cannot expect any measure of success against the well-established giants in either field.

Then, too, the name *Webster* can and has been borrowed for other fields. There are such "Webster's" as *Webster's American Military Biographies, Webster's Guide to Abbreviations, Webster's New World Secretarial Handbook*, and a direct-marketing glossary titled *Wiland's Webster*.

CHAPTER 7

ENCYCLOPEDIAS, HANDBOOKS, AND OTHER SPECIALIZED WORKS

✓ TITLING ENCYCLOPEDIAS

"With regard to the titling of encyclopedias," says Kenneth Kister,* an authority on encyclopedias, "you don't have the same problems as you do with dictionaries, where the names *Webster* and *Roget* dominate.

"In the encyclopedia field, marketing studies have established that the two most highly regarded are *World Book* and *Encyclopaedia Britannica*.

"One publisher came up with a name that would establish theirs as the first to be listed in any alphabetical list of encyclopedias. They started with the word *Academic*, figuring it was unlikely that any other encyclopedia could come up with a lower letter combination than 'Ac,' which is how their encyclopedia came to be called the *Academic American Encyclopedia*.

"What criteria are essential in selecting a name for an encyclopedia? If you're about to choose a name for an encyclopedia, you want a name that sounds good, is authoritative, and is recognized by the public.

"It was with these criteria in mind that the encyclopedia published by Random House came to be called the *Random House Encyclopedia*. The name *Random House* carries a certain amount of authority with the American public. The name *Webster* may be used often for dictionaries, but the name *Random House* cannot be misused."

To reinforce Kister's last point, it is a relatively frequent practice to differentiate an encyclopedia with a publisher identifier. Other examples of this include the *McGraw-Hill Encyclopedia of Science and Technology*, and the *New Caxton Encyclopedia*.

---

*Kenneth F. Kister is a veteran librarian, teacher, and author of several books and numerous articles on reference book evaluation, including *Best Encyclopedias: A Guide to General and Specialized Encyclopedias* (1986), and *Kister's Concise Guide to Best Encyclopedias* (1988), Phoenix: The Oryx Press.

A variant of this (harking back to Webster and Roget) is inclusion of an author identifier in the title. An example is the *Encyclopedia of Chemical Technology*, edited by Kirk and Othmer, which over 30 years in two editions was known to the chemical industry as "Kirk-Othmer." When the third edition initiated publication in 1978, it was retitled the *Kirk-Othmer Encyclopedia of Chemical Technology*.

✓ MULTIPLE-SUBJECT ENCYCLOPEDIAS: TITLING BY THEME

Many specialized encyclopedias are devoted to a single subject or discipline, usually covering all its topics in an A-to-Z arrangement. When issued simultaneously in multiple volumes, each volume usually contains an approximately equal number of pages.

But when an encyclopedia covers a number of distinctly different themes, dividing the encyclopedia by theme, with thematic titling for each volume, should be considered.

This is the opinion of Moshe Sachs, creator and editor of the *Worldmark Encyclopedia of the Nations*, now in its seventh edition and a worldwide library reference.

"I published the first edition of *Worldmark/Nations* as a single volume. But when I saw how it was being used, I divided the encyclopedia into five volumes continentally" [i.e., 1. United Nations; 2. Africa; 3. Americas; 4. Asia and Oceania; 5. Europe].

"It is my conviction that the use should dictate the titling of an encyclopedia. Obviously if you have an *Encyclopaedia Britannica*, you divide the volumes by signatures. But title identification should take into account *how* the encyclopedia is used and *who* will be using it.

"I'd like to illustrate this point by citing a legal encyclopedia I came across some 15 or so years ago. It consisted of 11 or 12 volumes and was divided by theme. I recall that the thickest volume had about 1,500 pages and the thinnest—about outer space—had only about 128 pages."

Incidentally—or perhaps not so coincidentally—the overall set title, *Worldmark Encyclopedia of the Nations*, was an excellent choice for precisely identifying the work's thematic content. Worldmark avoided an ambiguous title such as "International Encyclopedia" (though it was the original working title), wisely choosing a precise title that accurately and very specifically indicates just what the encyclopedia covers.

✔ GUIDELINES FOR USE OF *HANDBOOK* OR *ENCYCLOPEDIA* IN A TITLE

When titling reference works, there is often a strong inclination to include the words "Handbook of" or "Encyclopedia of" in the title. But before adding such words to a book's title, it is important to ensure that the book fulfills the premise of each type of work.

First of all, the terms "Encyclopedia" and "Handbook" are not interchangeable. Both serve entirely different purposes, although, in some instances in the past, works were sometimes labeled a *handbook* if mainly for purchase by individuals and an *encyclopedia* if mainly for purchase by librarians.

Dr. Martin Grayson, who was editor-in-chief of the *Kirk-Othmer Encyclopedia of Chemical Technology* (Wiley, 1985), one of the world's most widely used technical references, offers these primary differences:

> A handbook is usually organized along structural lines characteristic of its field. It contains, primarily, factual information, such as tables, lists, and charts, and is designed for the specialist in the subject. It is usually difficult for a nonspecialist to use to obtain an overview of a part of the subject. Even with an index, a handbook is often cryptic, full of jargon, and patched together with excerpts from primary literature references.

> An encyclopedia is organized as a dictionary, with alphabetical entries so that the subject can be easily accessed by keywords. Each review is self-standing and complete as coverage of that aspect of the subject. It will give data and hard information as illustrative material to help the reader understand the important aspects of the subject and also provide references as to where the remaining data can be found. The encyclopedia is designed to provide easy access by alphabetical entry with appropriate cross references to further facilitate locating related subject matter. It is edited carefully for use by the nonspecialist.

In summing up the basic differences between handbooks and encyclopedias, Grayson says encyclopedias, which sometimes cost thousands of dollars, will often be found in libraries, where they are considered reference tools. Handbooks, on the other hand, are rarely found anyplace but on the specialist's desk.

✔ TITLING ENCYCLOPEDIA SPINOFFS

A number of publishers of multivolume reference works and encyclopedias publish concise or other types of spinoff volumes from the larger multivolume works. Frequently, mention of the parent work is minimal—or entirely absent.

The *McGraw-Hill Encyclopedias of Physics, Astronomy, Chemistry and Engineering*, for example, make no mention of being spunoff from the larger parent title—the classic *McGraw-Hill Encyclopedia of Science and Technology*—on either jacket or binding. Nor does Wiley's *Concise Encyclopedia of Psychology* make similar mention of its four-volume parent work.

Wiley's *Kirk-Othmer Concise Encyclopedia of Chemical Technology*, while carrying no identification of its parent volume on the binding, does on its jacket under the title, where it is identified as "an authoritative abridgement of the 26-volume Kirk-Othmer Third Edition."

Columbia University Press's *Concise Columbia Encyclopedia* does not mention on either jacket or cover its derivation from the *Columbia Encyclopedia*, although the parent version is mentioned in the preface.

✓ ADDING *ENCYCLOPEDIA* TO PROFESSIONAL BOOK TITLE: POTENTIAL PROBLEM

Occasionally the word "Encyclopedia" is added to a professional book title to emphasize its scope, a practice that can lead to problems.

Some presses have encyclopedia discounts that differ from those for other types of professional books. By adding the word "Encyclopedia" to a title, the possibility always exists that the shipping facility may bill at the encyclopedia discount rate, which usually is lower than the discount afforded professional books. This can create problems with jobber and bookseller accounts.

Accordingly, when "Encyclopedia" is added to the title of a professional book, special care should be given to ensure that it will be treated the same as other professional books in the billing cycle.

✓ TITLING HANDBOOKS: TRADITIONAL AND NONTRADITIONAL METHODS

Traditionally a handbook title requires no elaboration beyond its subject (e.g., *Handbook of Industrial Engineering*), since it is presumed that the typical reader will have some knowledge of the subject and will turn to it only when specific information is needed.

However, when a compilation of information is designed to appeal to a varied nonspecialist audience and bears a "Handbook" label, it may be helpful to add an explanatory subtitle that will provide more information on its content (e.g., *The Copy-To-Press Handbook: Preparing Words for Art and Print*).

✔ WORD PATTERNS AND CONSTRUCTION IN HANDBOOK TITLING

As a rule, when a reference title starts with "Handbook" as the lead-off word, it is followed by "of" and then identifies the book's subject. The two alternatives to "of," though used infrequently, do serve a specific purpose. Occasionally, one will want to start with "Handbook for" and identify the intended audience rather than the content, as in *Handbook for Writers*. On rare occasions, "Handbook in" is useful in a subdiscipline or subfield of a scientific discipline, as in *Handbook in Diagnostic-Prescriptive Teaching*.

In those infrequent instances where a subtitle is called for (see preceding entry), the three most frequently used with handbooks are:

1. *A Guide to* (indicating subject or differentiation from competitive work)
2. *A Guide for* (indicating the intended audience or sometimes the subject)
3. *A Text and Reference for* (indicating both level and audience)

✔ HANDBOOK TITLING WHEN THERE ARE COMPETITIVE WORKS

When a handbook is an entry into a field where others already exist, the common titling practice is to label the handbook with a name identifier—either the original editor or the name of the publisher—to give it a unique identity. Here are examples of handbooks with their own identifiers:

+ *Lesly's Public Relations Handbook*
+ *Perry's Chemical Engineers Handbook*
+ *Standard Handbook for Civil Engineers*
+ *MLA Handbook for Writers of Research Papers*

✔ REFERENCE BOOK TITLING: ALTERNATIVE WORDS FOR *HANDBOOK*

If you're working on a title and you're considering "Handbook" as part of the title, you may want to consider the many alternative words that will serve just as well and give your title a somewhat different thrust—especially if works with the word "Handbook" in them already exist in the same subject area:

Advisor	Guidebook
Almanac	Library
Answer Book	Primer
Casebook	Reference
Companion	Resource Book
Compendium	Review
Course Book	Sourcebook
Desk Reference	Survey
Directory	Text/Textbook
Guide	Workbook
Ideabook	Yearbook

✓ REFERENCE BOOKS: WORDS FOR ADDED TITLE IMPACT

Once you've decided on what you want to call your reference book—dictionary, handbook, guide, manual, reference, or whatever—you may want to add another word to give the title more meaning or a better indication of its direction, level, or scope. Here are some "starter" examples:

To indicate size or scope:

Abridged	Comprehensive
Compact	Encyclopedic
Complete	Exhaustive
Concise	Expanded

To indicate level of presentation:

Advanced	Intermediate
Basic	Introductory
Elementary	Self-Study
Essentials of	Self-Teaching
Fundamentals of	

To indicate authority:

Authoritative	Original
Official	Standard

To indicate type of coverage:

Applied	In-Depth
Balanced	Nonmathematical
Complete	Objective
Current	Practical
Definitive	Systematic
Encyclopedic	Unified
Heavily Illustrated	Well-Documented

✔ **TITLING CONFERENCE AND SYMPOSIUM PROCEEDINGS**

Titling is not a major concern for conference of symposium proceedings, since such works generally take the name of the conference or incorporate the name of the conference into the subtitle. In rare instances where the conference is in a breakthrough area of science or technology, the title may consist of only the subject of the conference, with no identification in the title of its being a conference proceeding. *Machine Intelligence 10*, for example, would be the total cover title for the tenth conference on machine intelligence held at the University of Edinburgh.

There is, however, a caveat to such title abridgment. Many library approval plans, in their ordering profiles to library jobbers, specify "no conference proceedings." Consequently, it is useful to identify such publications as conference proceedings in the title or subtitle to avoid returns.

CHAPTER 8

TRAVEL GUIDES AND BOOKS, COOKBOOKS, AND ART BOOKS

✓ PROPER NAMES AS TRAVEL GUIDE TITLES: THE SERIES GIANTS

There are over a dozen successful travel guide series, each usually identifiable by a single "authority" name followed by the locale of the guide—usually a country, or sometimes a major city. The dominant series have such names as Frommer, Fielding, Fodor, Michelin, Birnbaum, and Baedeker. In fact, so ingrained is the name *Baedeker*—the oldest of the continuously published guides—that it is not uncommon for someone in explaining the completeness of a work to describe it as "a veritable Baedeker." The *Baedeker* name appears in most dictionaries as a word symbolizing travel guides.

There is no denying that these series dominate the travel field. But competition is possible—with the right title—as the next sections show.

✓ TRAVEL GUIDE TITLING: THE APPEAL TO SPECIAL INTERESTS

To a large extent, travel guides still bear simple one-word place names such as *Fodor's Hungary*, *Fodor's Portugal*, and *Fodor's Madrid*.

But the titles of today's travel guides are beginning to get away from places alone and to appeal to travelers' specialized interests as well. There are literally hundreds of guides tailored to special audiences and interests, such as:

✦ *The Discount Guide for Travelers Over 55*
✦ *The Executive's Guide to China*
✦ *Great American Scenic Railroads*
✦ *Fishing Hotspots: A Directory of the Best Places to Fish*
✦ *Ski Guide to North America*

Along with the place and subject guides, you find language-aid guides such as the *Chinese/English Phrase Book for Travelers.*

The rule for travel book titles seems to be: nothing fancy—just the facts.

✓ TRAVEL GUIDE TITLING: REGIONAL APPEAL

Although competing with the big-name series is an uphill battle, you will get more serious attention from booksellers and chain buyers with titles dealing with a specific region or group of regions.

People traveling to California, for example, are more likely to buy a "Guide to Bed and Breakfast Inns in Southern California" than a similar guide of national scope in which Southern California occupies only a small amount of space. And, of course, independent booksellers in California will find books dealing with their localized regions a "must" for in-store stock.

One publisher who follows the regional practice with great success is The East Woods Press of Charlotte, North Carolina, whose titles include:

✦ *The Jersey Shore—A Travel and Pleasure Guide*

✦ *Walking from Inn to Inn—The San Francisco Bay Area*

✦ *Virginia: Off the Beaten Path*

✓ GUIDE SERIES TAKES NAME OF NOTED TRAVEL AUTHORITY: CASE STUDY

Houghton Mifflin has built a successful travel guide series around the name of a single travel authority. The authority is Stephen Birnbaum, the most readily recognized travel authority in the United States.

Birnbaum's credentials are based on regular travel features on the TV show *Good Morning America,* daily newscasts on CBS radio, a monthly travel column in *Good Housekeeping* magazine, and a nationally syndicated newspaper column on what's new and best in the travel world.

Houghton Mifflin issues various titles with Birnbaum's name as the most prominent part of the title, followed by the area covered and the year. There are annual revisions for each volume in the paperback series.

Series titles include, each with current year added as part of title, *Birnbaum's Caribbean, Birnbaum's Hawaii, Birnbaum's Mexico, Birnbaum's South America, Birnbaum's Canada, Birnbaum's Europe, Birnbaum's France, Birnbaum's Great Britain and Ireland,* and *Birnbaum's United States.*

The Birnbaum name is the largest word on each of the covers, spanning nearly 4½" of the 5" cover width and with two heavy bands of color under the name to prominently set it off.

✓ TRAVEL BOOKS ARE NOT TRAVEL GUIDES: SOME TRAVEL BOOK TITLES

A travel book is not the same as a travel guide. The guide offers advice to travelers. The travel book represents an account of some travel activity or destination and is designed for pleasurable reading or browsing.

A selection of currently popular travel books, listed under the heading "Books for the Armchair Traveler" in the December 1, 1987, *Wall Street Journal,* included these titles:

✦ *The Norton Book of Travel*
✦ *The Amundsen Photographs*
✦ *A Walk to the Pole*
✦ *Prairiescapes*
✦ *A Day in the Life of the Soviet Union*
✦ *A Country House Companion*
✦ *English Country: Living in England's Private Homes*
✦ *Shakespeare Country*

✓ CHOOSING A COOKBOOK TITLE: SOME SALES-BUILDING GUIDELINES

When selecting a cookbook title, sometimes the author's name in the title will help sales; for example, *Beard on Bread.*

Sometimes the title sells the cookbook; for example, *The Enchanted Broccoli Forest, The Pasta Salad Book, Cold Soups,* and *The Chocolate Cookbook.*

But beware! There is a fine line between terrific and disastrously cute. Avoid a title so original it completely obscures the book's intent. What you must aim for is a title that is both memorable and descriptive.

This, in part, is the advice of Hayes, Rolfes & Associates in their *How to Write and Publish a Classic Cookbook*, published by New American Library, 1986.

✓ ALL-TIME BESTSELLING HARDCOVER COOKBOOKS

Cookbooks are said to be the steadiest bestsellers since the advent of printing, second only to the Bible in sales with over 400 new titles entering the market each year. Tops among the most successful cookbooks is *The Betty Crocker Cookbook*, a title that has led the field in cookbook sales for more than 40 years. Below is a complete list of the top ten hardcover bestsellers.*

1. *The Betty Crocker Cookbook*, 1950 (22,000,000)
2. *Better Homes & Gardens New Cookbook*—Ringbound, 1930 (20,685,435).
3. *The Joy of Cooking*, 1931 (10,000,000).
4. *Mr. Boston Bartender's Guide*, 1935 (8,659,686).
5. *Better Homes and Gardens New Garden Book*, 1959 (2,526,953).
6. *Better Homes and Gardens New Junior Cook Book*, 1975 (1,652,417).
7. *Better Homes and Gardens Cooking for Two*, 1968 (1,585,418).
8. *Weight Watchers International Cookbook*, 1980 (1,245,000).
9. *Better Homes and Gardens Home Canning and Freezing*, 1973 (1,152,372).
10. *Better Homes and Gardens Barbecue Cook Book*, 1956 (1,148,612).

✓ MILLION-SELLING PAPERBACK COOKBOOKS†

Paperback cookbooks that have sold more than a million copies include:

---

*Adapted from: *Book Publishing Annual*, 1985 Edition, New York: R.R. Bowker. Omitted is *Better Homes and Gardens Fondue Book*, a 1970 title now out of print that would have ranked 9th, with 1,484,278. Also not included is *The Frugal Gourmet*, a title that exceeded one million copies in sales in the fall of 1987.

† From: *Book Publishing Annual*, 1985 Edition, New York: R.R. Bowker.

✦ *Crockery Cookery*, 1975
✦ *The Nutrition Almanac*, 1979
✦ *Joy of Cooking*, 1973
✦ *Mexican Cook Book*, 1969
✦ *Barbecue Cook Book*, 1938
✦ *Breads*, 1963
✦ *Wok Cookery*, 1977
✦ *Crepe Cookery*, 1976
✦ *Favorite Recipes*, 1949
✦ *Canning*, 1975
✦ *Oriental Cook Book*, 1970
✦ *Hors D'Oeuvres*, 1976
✦ *Make-a-Mix Cookery*, 1978

✔ TITLING APPROACHES TO COMPETE WITH THE BIGTIME COOKBOOKS

It is sometimes hard to compete against *Betty Crocker* and other successful cookbooks that sell in the tens of thousands year after year. But there is a way for the smaller houses or regional publishers to compete.

Begin by heeding the advice given by Barbara Anderson of St. Martin's Press, editor of the *Great American Peanutbutter Book*: "The trick is to locate a food passion and then [title] a book on the subject which will appeal to the impulse buyer" (*Publishers Weekly*, September 20, 1985).

This advice can be translated into developing thematic or regional titles and building your cookbook around it. There are untold possibilities for both, as evidenced by these recent examples:

✦ *Cajun Cooking*
✦ *Down Home Southern Cooking*
✦ *General Electric Microwave Guide and Cookbook*
✦ *The Mexican Salt-Free Diet Cookbook*
✦ *Chinese Cooking for Beginners*
✦ *A Taste of India*
✦ *The Starving Students' Cookbook*

✓ TWENTY POSSIBLE THEMES FOR COOKBOOK TITLING

Here are some thematic possibilities for cookbook titling:

1. Microwave Cooking
2. Ethnic Food
3. Diet/Low Calorie
4. Baking
5. Gourmet
6. Vegetable/Vegetarian
7. Appliance Other than Microwave
8. Barbecue
9. Quick Meals
10. Bread
11. Canning/Freezing
12. Meat
13. Casserole
14. Hors d'Oeuvres/Party
15. Cooking for One or Two
16. Pasta
17. Fish/Seafood
18. Soup
19. Children's
20. General

✓ CATCHY COOKBOOK SELLS NEARLY 700,000 ON TITLE ALONE

Let's Cook Microwave, published by Barbara Harris Inc., a small press in Portland, Oregon,* has sold more than 700,000 copies in its ten years in print—all with no advertising whatsoever. So reports John Kremer in *Book Marketing Update* (February 1987).

"Yes," says Kremer, "they've never advertised, yet they still receive 200 to 300 mail orders every week, all from word of mouth. The book is also distributed to bookstores. When the spiral-bound $7.95 book goes back to press, they print 50,000 copies at a time."

---

*Barbara Harris Inc., P.O. Box 2992, Portland, OR 97208.

✔ SLIGHT TITLE CHANGE ENABLES MODEST-SELLING COOKBOOK TO TOP 300,000

Consumer attitudes are no less important in the cookbook field than in other areas, as John Storey of Garden Way/Storey Communications explains.

At the 1987 Association of American Publishers Symposium on Trade Book Publishing, Storey talked about product improvement based on consumer tests. As an example, he told of a book published as *The Squash Book*, which sold 1,500 copies. The book cover was redesigned and the book reissued with a new title, *The Zucchini Cookbook*, which now has more than 300,000 copies in print.

✔ ART BOOKS: TITLING PATTERNS

Based on a seasonal announcement of forthcoming art books from 59 publishers in the September 15, 1987, *Library Journal*, it appears that a few of these publishers include the word "art" in their titles, such as:

◆ *The Art of Rock*
◆ *The Art of Seeing Animals*
◆ *The Theatre Art of Boris Aronson*

Approximately 50 percent of the titles of all publishers were lengthy and compound, with the two parts separated by a colon. Surprisingly, a number of the compound titles repeated a descriptive word in both halves of the title, as these examples demonstrate:

◆ *The Naked and the Nude: A History of the Nude in Photographs*
◆ *The Building of Manhattan: How Manhattan Was Built Overground and Underground, from the Dutch Settlers to the Skyscrapers*
◆ *Pasta Classica: The Art of Italian Pasta Cooking*

At least a dozen of the compound titles had the name of an artist or illustrator as the first half, with the explanatory statement of the title following the colon.

Art titles also tend to run long.

CHAPTER 9

RELIGIOUS BOOKS

✓ DEFINITION OF A RELIGIOUS BOOK

What is a religious book? It might be a book on a religious theme; it might be a book of spiritual or inspirational values. Perhaps the best definition I've seen was by Eugene Exman, a former vice-president of Harper & Row in charge of religious publishing.

Exman defines religious books, in *What Happens in Book Publishing* (2nd ed., Columbia University Press, 1967), as "Books published by religious book specialists, reviewed and advertised largely in religious periodicals, and sold through religious book outlets to people interested in religion."

✓ TITLE CRITERIA FOR RELIGIOUS BOOK CLUB OFFERINGS

"What do you look for in a title for your religious book club?" we asked the editor of one such club.

Replied the editor, "We look for three things in the title of a book offering: (1) it has to say what the book is about, (2) it has to be religious, and (3) it has to have an inspirational lift.

"There have been occasions," she added, "where we liked a book but not its title and, with permission of the publisher and author, we offered the book with a changed title. But, in general, the religious market is a very specific market. We like a religious title to be a little 'catchy' but not too clever and in general tell our club members what's in the book."

✓ TITLING PATTERNS, KEYS, AND DIFFERENCES IN VARIOUS RELIGIOUS MARKETS

What constitutes a good religious book title? Again we asked the question—this time of Barbara Kolbe of Servant Publications in Ann Arbor, Michigan. Servant publishes books of practical Christian teaching, theology, inspirational content, and Scripture study.

"It depends," says Ms. Kolbe, "on which religious market you are talking about. In the evangelical Protestant market, for example, your title has to be real upbeat and not too heavy. You have to put a bit of Christian religiousness into it. Your title has to offer hope.

"You have to include strong words—like 'learning,' 'close,' 'near,' 'loving,' 'feeling,' and 'freedom.' 'Prayer' is a big word for titles in the religious book market.

"Now for the Catholic market, there are different types of words that do well in titles—words such as 'selection,' 'encounter,' 'motherhood,' 'family,' 'miracles,' 'contemplative,' and 'Scripture'. We use 'Scripture' more than 'Bible' for the Catholic market. Also, we like to use the word 'Saint' in a title when it is appropriate. 'Suffering' is a word that works well for titles for both the Catholic and Protestant markets. Another word we use a lot in titles is 'you', though mostly in subtitles.

"How does the Catholic market differ from other religious markets? Well, for one thing, books for the Catholic market tend to have the word 'Catholic' in the title, or else somewhere in the subtitle. If a Catholic wants to read something Catholic, they want to be able to find it in the book's title. I would say that that's the number one requirement for a Catholic book title.

"Another thing that helps sell Catholic books and to reinforce the title is a quote on the cover or jacket from a prominent Catholic churchman or layperson.

"In religious book publishing," Ms. Kolbe concludes, "books really sell by author, the author's name being more important than the title. In the religious world, books often sell by author and by publishing house. Many people buy religious books on the reputation of the publishing house, though that tendency has been breaking down lately."

✓ RELIGIOUS BOOK TITLING PATTERNS

A study was made of titling patterns in the seasonal religious book announcements of 71 publishers, involving 385 different titles.

The most common pattern in religious book titling is in the frequency of certain key words. Of the 385 titles studied, the most frequently used words were "Bible" or "Biblical." They appeared in 25 titles.

Tied for second place close behind the leaders were "God" and "Christian," appearing in 23 titles each. Here are the study results:

1. *Bible/Biblical* 25
2. *God, Christian* .... 23 each

3. *Church, Religious/Religion, Jewish/Judaism* .... 9 each
4. *Jesus, Catholic/Catholicism, Prayers/Prayer* .... 6 each
5. *Child/Children* .... 5 each
6. *Christ, Old Testament* .... 4 each
7. *Spiritual* .... 3 each
8. *New Testament, Gospel, Women, Marriage* .... 2 each
9. *Heaven, Sermons, Worship* .... 1 each

Of the 385 titles studied, 111 (approximately 29 percent) were compound titles divided by a colon. Approximately 1 percent more were compound, but divided by dashes.

Twelve titles asked a question (*How Can We Know?; Is That in the Bible?*), with 11 including a question mark as part of the title. Five of the 385 included the words "Dictionary of" in their titles.

✓ COMMON INGREDIENTS OF MANY BIBLE DICTIONARY TITLES

Although the Bible is the world's biggest seller, there are not nearly as many Bibles as there are dictionaries of the Bible. A count in *Books in Print* indicated approximately 125 such dictionaries.

While *Bible Dictionary* or *Dictionary of the Bible* are fairly common, a goodly percentage lead off their titles with the name of the Bible dictionary's compiler. Thus, you'll find Boyd's, Cruden's, Davis, Meredith's, Smith's, Unger's, Wilson's, and Young's Bible dictionaries.

You will also find that a number of religious publishers identify their edition of the Bible dictionary with the name of their publishing establishment. Thus, you'll also find dictionaries with Revell's, New Westminster or Westminster, Oxford, and Zondervan as the lead title word or words.

As with other types of dictionaries, larger versions sometimes have smaller spinoff or concise versions. *Unger's Bible Dictionary*, for example, has a massive 1,200-page cloth version, as well as a much reduced-in-size *Unger's Concise Bible Dictionary* in paperback for $4.95.

✓ SUCCESSFUL RELIGIOUS TITLES OF THE PAST

In religious publishing, titles in past years that have achieved great popularity, sold in the millions, and made the various bestseller lists have frequently rallied around a single theme and started with "The." Some prominent examples are:

✦ The Song of Bernadette
✦ The Robe
✦ The Keys of the Kingdom
✦ The Apostle
✦ The Bishop's Mantle
✦ The Big Fisherman
✦ The Razor's Edge
✦ The Beloved Country
✦ The Cardinal
✦ The Prophet
✦ The Man from Nazareth
✦ The Screwtape Letters

✓ TITLING BOOKS WITH CONTROVERSIAL THEMES: THE CROSSWAY APPROACH

Crossway Books in Westchester, Illinois, is a religious publisher that deals in books on controversial issues.

"We are not afraid of controversy, says Jan Dennis, editor-in-chief of Crossway. "We take on controversial issues and try to give them a Christian, authoritative perspective.

"Insofar as book titling is concerned," adds Dennis, "we follow a policy of 'truth in titling'—what we try to do is come up with a title that accurately depicts a book's content. But we also consider it important not to slavishly adhere to that principle. What we try to do in that 'accurate' description is to figure a way to have the title make an impact on the potential reader.

"Titling of religious books is quite different from what a secular publisher might do. We try to get a title that has some kind of biblical overtone—possibly use a quote from the Bible that will strike a chord.

"Most of the books that Crossway publishes are (1) confrontational, (2) informational, and (3) motivational. We don't fit very much into the mold of your typical religious publisher.

"In our titling, we try to create an aura of combativeness. One example is a book by Mary Pride that is doing very nicely for us at this time: The Child Abuse Industry: Outrageous Facts About Child Abuse and Everyday Rebellion Against a System That's Threatened Every North American Family.

"The title is pretty long, but it tells the story: the book is more about the child-abuse bureaucracy and not about the subject itself. The author believes the public is using hysteria to interfere with parental control of the family."

✓ DIFFICULT BOOK TO TITLE: AUTHOR FINDS SOLUTION IN BIBLICAL PARABLE

A well-known theologian was writing a book on religion and politics, although neither the author nor his editor could think of an appropriate title. The priest turned to the Bible and found the solution to his problem in Matthew 22:15-22.

The parable therein ends with Jesus telling the Pharisees, "Then give to Caesar what is Caesar's, but give to God what is God's." He decided to call his book *Caesar's Coin: Religion and Politics in America*, and the book's jacket bore an enlarged illustration of a gold coin of Augustus Caesar. The 1987 title from Macmillan had a highly successful launch. Author Richard P. McBrien is a past president of the Catholic Theological Society of America and chairs the department at the University of Notre Dame.

CHAPTER 10

CHILDREN'S BOOKS

✓ DEFINITION OF A CHILDREN'S BOOK

"What is a children's book?" Ann Beneduce, former editorial director of Philomel Books, a Young Readers Group imprint of Putnam Publishing, provides an apt description:*

"Children's books cover a broad area. Children as an audience range from newborn infants to high school seniors. For the tiniest infants there are cloth or board books to play with, chew on, take into the bathtub, or sleep with, as well as picture books and stories for parents to read aloud.

"Then come more complex picture books and 'easy readers' for the 6-, 7- and 8-year olds just beginning to read independently. Next come the 8-to-11s, the so-called middle-aged children who want more grown-up looking books, fairly simple to read but offering a broad spectrum of subjects, both informational and in fiction.

"The category once named 'teenage books' is now read by this pre-teenaged audience, while teenagers read what are called 'young adult' or 'YA' books, which are becoming more and more similar in subject matter to adult books, but with the protagonists still in their teens."

✓ CHILDREN'S BOOK TITLING: VIEWS OF A SENIOR EDITOR

"Titling for children's books pretty much follows the formula for adult titles. You want a title that is arresting, intriguing—something that will make the reader curious," says Bonnie Ingber, senior editor for children's books at Harcourt Brace Jovanovich in San Diego.

"The children's publishing program at HBJ covers everything from toddlers to teens and it is my feeling that a picture book title could work just as well for a novel, if it is a good one.

"What constitutes a good title? One that reflects the spirit of the book.

---

*From: *Book Publishing Career Directory* edited by Ronald W. Fry, Hawthorne, NJ: The Career Press.

"An example of a children's title I like, and, by the way, one that is also doing very well saleswise, is HBJ's *Growing Vegetable Soup*. It's for children aged 3 to 6 and it is about growing vegetables that are made into soup.

"That title was from the author, and it has worked well. However, not all titles suggested by authors work that well. When we find a title we have difficulty with, we talk it out among ourselves here at HBJ and then send a suggested list of alternates to the author. It is the writer, however, who makes the final decision. Titling has never been a problem because we try to go along with the author's wishes."

✓ CHILDREN'S BOOK TITLES: VIEWS OF A VETERAN SCHOOL LIBRARIAN

"One of the things that troubles me about children's book titles," says Dorothy Blake, coordinator of libraries for the Atlanta school system and a veteran children's librarian of some 30 years, "is that so many authors and editors are so intent on giving us titles that are cute and clever that you wind up having no idea what the book is about.

"A case in point is a title in a bibliography I am currently working on. The title is *Callooh! Callay!* The book is from Atheneum. Fortunately, there is a subtitle, *Holiday Poems for Young Readers*. If it weren't for the subtitle, one would be at a loss to understand this title.

"If you want some advice for publishers of children's books, tell them somewhere, somehow, in their book there has to be a relationship between something clever and something that gives you a clue as to what the book is about."

✓ TITLES WITH CHILD APPEAL: VIEWS OF A PUBLIC LIBRARIAN

"The type of book titles with the greatest appeal for children in the fourth, fifth, sixth, and seventh grades are those that are both funny and catchy."

The speaker is Lynn Pickens, head of the Children's Department at the Atlanta Fulton Public Library.

"That type of title," adds Ms. Pickens, "makes more of a difference than other types of titles, and they're always popular with the kids. Two especially popular titles I can think of are *The Cat Ate My Gymsuit* and *Nothing's Fair in Fifth Grade.*

"Another useful idea in children's book titling is to get the lead character's name into the title if the book is part of a series. One popular series is the Encyclopedia Brown books; another is the Ramona books. Kids love series, and if they like one book in the series, they'll want to look at the others in the same series.

"I don't have any turnoffs insofar as children's book titles are concerned, but I do think that anyone who is thinking about titling of children's books should avoid including in their titles any trendy words such as 'Yuppies.' Children's titles have to appeal for a long time, and a children's title should avoid any word that might become dated.

"Title is incidental to me, but to the children its an entirely different matter. Children look at titles and the book's title helps them to make a decision."

✓ SMALL-COMMUNITY CHILDREN'S LIBRARIANS GIVE VIEWS ON TITLES

"When you think of titles for children's books, you have to remember there are a number of different categories of children's books, and requirements vary with different age levels."

The speaker is Melanie Axel-Lute, the children's librarian at the South Orange Public Library, a suburban New Jersey community of approximately 15,000 population, with a 93,000-volume collection.

Librarian Axel-Lute agrees with librarian Pickens (in the preceding section) that children in grades four to six like weird and funny titles, adding, "It's a good idea to bear in mind that between the cover and the title, kids make up their minds about a book very quickly. I think it's very good for children's books to have funny titles."

She also agrees with Pickens on the importance of including the series name in the title, but adds one proviso:

"One problem that I often encounter in children's books is books by the same author in the same series that are very similar in both sound and spelling. A good example are these two titles by Donald Sobol: *Encyclopedia Brown Takes the Cake* and *Encyclopedia Brown Takes the Case*. There are a number of children's series where titles are very similar. Perhaps publishers do this because it helps the children to more readily identify the titles as being part of a particular series.

"Of course if you're thinking of titles for very young readers, you're best off with a one- or two-word title. I'm talking about children from preschool to second grade. Kids remember the very short titles much better."

The children's librarians in two adjacent small communities—at the Maplewood and Orange libraries—confirm librarians Axel-Lute's and Pickens's opinions relative to children favoring funny, weird, or catchy titles. They also liked the idea of having the series name or lead character in the title for ease of identification.

One librarian cautioned authors of children's books to avoid including words from an unfamiliar quotation, or, for that matter, any word in a title that would be unfamiliar to children. "Kids are quick to reject such titles," she said.

✓ THE IMPORTANCE OF SERIES NAMES OVER INDIVIDUAL TITLES

The mass-market publishers of children's books tend to concentrate on series and, in some cases, as with the Golden Books, a series life may span generations.

A key reason for the popularity of series in children's books is the way in which many children's books are bought. A parent buys a book for a child, say a Golden Book, and it's a rousing success. Very likely that parent will eventually go back to where that first book was bought and look for another Golden Book, not for any particular title. Or the parent might suggest a Golden Book as something a child favors when asked for gift suggestions. The key, then, is that a series establishes a brand name identity.

The book-buying parents of children of reading age will often seek out series they recall from their own childhood, such as The Bobbsey Twins, Nancy Drew, The Hardy Boys, and Tom Swift.

✓ TITLING PATTERNS IN SUCCESSFUL CHILDREN'S SCIENCE SERIES

When it comes to science books for children, simple titles tied to focused themes win out, as exemplified by the Golden Press science guides, a topselling series for more than 40 years.

The 4″ x 6″ $3.95 paperback guides with text and illustrations, prepared by world renowned authorities and reflecting recent scientific developments, are recommended and used by untold thousands of science teachers.

Most guides bear simple one-word thematic titles such as: *Birds, Fishes, Flowers, Fossils, Geology.*

Titling of a few of the science guides run longer, but not one letter longer than is necessary to describe succinctly the guide's con-

tent. Some examples are *Butterflies and Moths, Pond Life,* and *Reptiles and Amphibians.*
Could it be said in any fewer words?

✔ THEMATIC TITLING: APPEALING TO CHILDREN'S SPECIAL INTERESTS

Just as many reference librarians seek out books in specific subject areas to enhance their collections, children who read also seek out books that enable them to broaden their knowledge within a single area.

Jean Karl of the Athenium Children's Books Division explains the phenomenon: "Children who read are eager to explore all areas, often one area at a time. [They may read] all the horse books they can find, then . . . all the 'electricity' books . . . then through all the science fiction, and so on."*

Such books can often be grouped and promoted by theme or subject, with one title helping sell the related ones.

✔ TITLE LENGTHS AND WORD PATTERNS IN BESTSELLING CHILDREN'S BOOKS

In a list of children's bestsellers, issued by Baker & Taylor, a leading supplier of children's books, the average title length of the top ten books was 4.4 words.

Analysis of these titles indicated the following among the 44 words comprising the ten titles:

✦ 7 of the 10 had *the* in the title
✦ 26 words (59%) were of one syllable
✦ 14 words (31%) were of two syllables
✦ 3 words (6.6%) were of three syllables
✦ 1 word (2.2%) was of four syllables

In the same release, there also appeared a listing of 17 major new children's releases from a variety of publishers. These new titles exhibited a strikingly similar word number and syllable pattern to those of the Baker & Taylor list of children's bestsellers.

In children's titles, virtually all words of more than one syllable are names of people, places, or things. In the above study, the multi-

---

*From: *What Happens in Book Publishing,* Second Edition, edited by Chandler B. Grannis, New York: Columbia University Press, 1967.

syllable words included *African, Washington, Constitution, Dictionary, Alexander,* and *Skyscraper*—words that while lengthy are generally recognizable and known to their readers.

✓ **TITLES OF BESTSELLING CHILDREN'S BOOKS BETWEEN 1895 AND 1973***

Green Eggs and Ham, Dr. Seuss, 1960	5,940,776
One Fish, Two Fish, Red Fish, Blue Fish, Dr. Seuss, 1963	5,842,024
Hop on Pop, Dr. Seuss, 1963	5,814,101
Dr. Seuss's ABC, Dr. Seuss, 1963	5,648,193
The Cat in the Hat, Dr. Seuss, 1957	5,394,741
The Wonderful Wizard of Oz, L. Frank Baum, 1900 (est.)	5,000,000
Charlotte's Web, E.B. White, 1952	4,670,516
The Cat in the Hat Comes Back, Dr. Seuss, 1958	3,431,917
The Little Prince, Antoine de Saint-Exupery, 1943	2,811,478
The Little House on the Prairie, Laura Ingalls Wilder, 1953	2,732,666
The Little House in the Big Woods, Laura Ingalls Wilder, editor, 1953	2,527,203
My First Atlas, 1959	2,431,000
Love and the Facts of Life, Evelyn Duvall and Sylvanus Duvall, 1950	2,360,000
Egermeier's Bible Story Book, Elsie E. Egermeier, 1923	2,326,577
Go Ask Alice, Anonymous, 1971	2,245,605
Benji, Leonore Fleischer, 1974	2.235,694
The Little Engine That Could, Watty Piper, 1926	2,166,000
Freckles, Gene Stratton Porter, 1904	2,089,523
The Girl of the Limberlost, Gene Stratton Porter, 1909	2,053,892

---

*From: *Eighty Years of Best Sellers* by A.P. Hackett and J.H. Burke, New York: R.R. Bowker, 1977. Includes books published in the U.S. from 1895 through 1973 that sold over 2 million copies.

CHAPTER 11

SCIENTIFIC, TECHNICAL, AND MEDICAL BOOKS

✓ CLASSIFICATIONS OF SCIENTIFIC BOOKS AND TITLING FOR EACH

Books classified as "scientific" generally fall into two classifications: those for a specialist audience, and those for the nonspecialist.

Titles for specialist books must be subject specific and identify the content with precision.

Titles for nonspecialist books often aim at younger audiences, and range from gardening and farming to astronomy and space exploration, from weather and health to natural history and social research. Nonspecialist science books should have titles that are simple and easy to grasp, reflecting their easy-to-understand text. Examples include *Thinking Machines, Volcanoes, Human Evolution, Life in the Universe,* and *Survival in Space.*

✓ WHY AUTHORS OF SCI-TECH BOOKS OFTEN NEED HELP WITH TITLING

The author of a scientific or technical book is usually of proven technical competence. Despite this, however, such an author is not a professional writer and, according to Curtis Benjamin,* "rarely even a skilled writer.

"As a rule he has little interest in matters of style. . . . Writing is his sideline and his livelihood is not involved. . . . Commonly he writes more for personal satisfaction or professional prestige than for the modest royalties his book may earn."

Although most pick a title closely tied to the book's content, many rely on jargon, on words of special meaning to only a few, or, occasionally, on their spouses and children. They are therefore often in need of counseling on titles from editors, publishers, and marketers.

---

*Curtis G. Benjamin in *What Happens in Book Publishing,* Second Edition, edited by Chandler B. Grannis, New York: Columbia University Press, 1967.

✔ CRITERIA FOR GOOD SCI-TECH BOOK TITLING*

A good sci-tech book title, according to Paul Edmonds, is one that satisfies these two criteria:

1. It should immediately and unambiguously convey what the book is about.
2. It should be readily indexable under a word that will occur to the reasonable inquirer.

"If the subject can be made part of the first word or two of the title, so much the better," adds Edmonds. Reasonable use of nouns in apposition (*Steel Frame Design Examples*) commends itself, though one can easily slip into horrible strings of them.

"I prefer the Saxon and the short, as against the classical and orotund, as a genuine sales advantage. I recall when we were about to publish the *Proceedings of a Symposium on the Composting of Sewage with Industrial Waste* (at Macmillan & Co., Ltd., London). I retitled it *Town Waste Put to Use*, and municipal authorities all over the world sent their orders for it."

Or consider a book titled *Knowing Everything About Nothing: Specialization and Change in Scientific Careers*. A much less ambiguous and indexable title would have been *Scientific Careers: Examining Specialization and Change*.

✔ IMPORTANCE OF BOOK TITLES: VIEWS OF LIBRARY MANAGER AT FORTUNE 300 COMPANY

How important are book titles to the manager of libraries for a Fortune 300 company with a collection mainly in science and technology?

The question was put to Deborah Kaufman, Manager, Corporate Libraries for the Perkin-Elmer Corporation in Norwalk, Connecticut.

"The title is going to be the first thing I see," says Ms. Kaufman, "because I do a lot of scanning [of many different publications]. The title tells me whether [the book] is something I'm interested in."

---

*Adapted from: "Nuts and Bolts" by Paul Edmonds, *Scholarly Publishing*, Vol. 3 (no. 1): October 1971. Edmonds was director of science and technology publishing at Macmillan & Co., Ltd., before his retirement in 1969.

"I'm always looking for titles that relate to the types of businesses my company is in. . . . I'm forced to scan because I do not have the time to sit down and read."

Ms. Kaufman was then asked if there are any kinds of titles that don't appeal to her.

"I don't like 'cutesy' titles. . . . It doesn't happen in the sci-tech area, but I'm getting to see more and more of it in the management area."

What role do titles play in the day-to-day operation of the Perkin-Elmer libraries?

"Titles are extremely important in how the people who use our libraries find out what we have. We circulate a library bulletin to 600 Perkin-Elmer managers and key employees on our distribution list and all we supply is the bibliographic information—subject, author, and title. The information is listed alphabetically by subject, and then alphabetically by author. But the titles stand alone; there is no added descriptive matter.

"I wish more publishers would realize how much importance a technical library such as ours places on book titles and devote more effort to making them meaningful enough for us to make good buying decisions, and for potential users of the books to be able to quickly ascertain what their contents offer."

✓ SCI-TECH BOOK TITLES MUST BE MEAN-INGFUL: HERE'S WHY

A key reason for effective, meaningful titles of sci-tech books is that the book sections of many scientific and scholarly periodicals include sections listing all new books received for review.

Readers scan these new book listings with great intensity to keep abreast of changing developments within their specialized areas and frequently, when a title is meaningful enough, will place an order on the strength of the listing. How many orders, for example, are going to come in for a book titled *One Medicine*, a book that might have been better titled *Cellular Function and Organismal Development: Similarity Among Animals* to reflect its subject matter?

It should be borne in mind by those responsible for titling that various branches of science and technology are undergoing rapid change. The title, therefore, should be as long as is necessary to accurately describe the book to those seeking or needing the information it offers.

An ongoing problem of short, incomplete titles is that by offering insufficient information, those ordering them frequently find the book not up to their needs or expectations and return the book. Accuracy in titling—no matter how many words are necessary—is often a book's most effective selling tool.

✔ ACRONYMS IN TITLES: WHEN TO USE OR NOT TO USE

A growing phenomenon in scientific and technical book titling is the use of acronyms without spelling out their meanings. This is a questionable practice, since many potential purchasers of these titles may be nonscientific or nontechnical personnel seeking reference sources. An explanation of the acronym would be helpful in identifying the subject matter of the book.

True, there are numerous acronyms that have become common and are universally recognized, *laser* being one, *VCR* another. *HPLC* is now fairly well recognized as meaning high-pressure liquid chromatography by most people who buy books in this field, as is *NMR* for nuclear magnetic resonance. Consequently most book titles in the two latter areas rarely use more than the acronym in the title.

A good titling rule of thumb: In mature fields, acronyms in titles are safe; in emerging fields, such as computer science, explain the acronym somewhere in the title or subtitle to be safe.

✔ BUILDING AUTHORITY INTO A SCI-TECH TITLE

When your scientific or technical book presents information that is based on expertise of a known or readily recognizable authority or source, it is useful to incorporate the source into the title. You thus give the potential buyer an implied "guarantee" that the information in the book can be taken at face value and that all the sources of the material it presents are reliable. Here are some examples:

IEEE Standard Dictionary of Electrical and Electronics Terms
The IEEE is the world's largest professional organization in these fields and considered the world's most reliable source in these areas.

ATA Type Comparison Book
The source is the Advertising Typographers Association, recognized as the professional organization of this field.

Elsevier's Oil and Gas Field Dictionary: In Six Languages
This publisher is recognized as the world's foremost publisher of multilingual technical dictionaries, and its name implies both quality of product and reliability of content.

✓ THE SPINE AS A FACTOR IN TITLING SCIENTIFIC BOOKS

"The book title should not be so long that it is hard to remember or hard to put on a book spine."

The speaker is a highly regarded editor of scientific and professional books in a New York science publishing establishment.

"Books are frequently identified on a shelf by their spine, and when the title is too long, the type must be very small and, therefore, the book is hard to identify and to recognize quickly when sandwiched in with others.

"A possible solution is a compound title with a short front and a longer back. The first name has to be something that is recognized by the majority of the book's potential audience and not just a 'zinger' that people will skip over."

✓ TITLING APPROACHES AND KEY WORDS FOR SELLING ENGINEERING BOOKS

Len Josephson, editor-in-chief of the McGraw-Hill Book Clubs, offers two useful guidelines for titling approaches if you want them to have appeal in engineering-related markets.

(1) Don't try to catch everybody in the title. If you can't, or if you do not want to in your main title, you can do it in the subtitle.

(2) If your book is directed to one particular group, or if your main market is one specific group, your sales will be better if the title is directed to that one specific audience. For example, don't use "Engineers and Architects"—you're better off if you limit the title wording to one specific group.

Josephson, who has had many years of experience managing book clubs in the various engineering disciplines, offers this advice on key words that have proven themselves to be sales-builders over the years.

"These words," says Josephson, "work amazingly well in the marketplace: *Applications, Calculations, Design, Practical,* and *Simplified.*"

He also offers these two bits of advice for successful titling of engineering books: (1) avoid coined words, and (2) be sure that whatever words you choose make it very clear what's in the book.

✔ BUILDING "SELL" INTO ENGINEERING BOOK TITLES: GUIDELINES

To build "sell" into a title, one must know what potential buyers are buying—and why. In the engineering field, there is some guidance for this available.

During a 1981 McGraw-Hill focus group discussion, six practicing engineers suggested three primary reasons why an engineer buys a book: (1) to help solve an immediate engineering problem; (2) to help update professional skills or knowledge; (3) to eliminate perceived job threats due to lack of knowledge.

Handbooks on specific subjects imply a wide compendium the engineer can turn to for needed information.

Building currentness into a title can be done, provided the contents merit it, by incorporating such words into the title as "Current"; for state-of-the-art works, "Modern," or "Recent," or listing a year or specified time span is useful.

Building broadness into coverage of books other than handbooks can be done by including in the title such words as "Comprehensive" or adding a subtitle with such words as "Sourcebook" or "Guidebook."

Building in the fact that the book's contents are useful in practice can be done by adding as a subtitle: *A Practical Guide, A Working Approach, Practical Applications,* or *Techniques.*

✔ THE MEDICAL BOOK MARKET: A BROAD OVERVIEW OF TITLING REQUIREMENTS

While considered a single specialist field, the medical book market is, in reality, more than a score of different medical specialties. Each is sufficiently distinct from the others to be a clearly defined discipline with its own titling requirements.*

Unless a book deals with broad generalities that apply to the practicing medical professional as a whole, a medical book title usually is targeted not only to the medical specialty for which it is written but also to a specific level or audience within that specialty.

As a general set of rules, titles for medical books should be in formal language if for practicing professionals, in less formal language if for students or as an introduction to a subject.

Textbook titles should endeavor to give an indication as to level (*Introduction to, Essentials of, Intermediate, Advanced,* etc.).

---

*From: *The Publisher's Direct Mail Handbook* by Nat Bodian, Philadelphia: ISI Press, 1987.

Following is a category-by-category set of suggestions for titling in the medical field:

Reference Books:
A reference book title should identify its subject.
Example: *The History of Surgical Anesthesia*

Clinical Texts:
This type of book is aimed at the doctor in practice, and the title should describe some technique or benefit or recent research result relative to the doctor's specialty.
Example: *Textbook of Clinical Anatomy*

Student Textbooks:
A student textbook should endeavor to include the level, if possible.
Examples: *Introduction to Neurosurgery; Advanced Hematology*

Atlases:
In an atlas format where the content is developed primarily by illustrations rather than by text, it is useful to start the title with *Atlas of* and then supply the subject.
Examples: *Atlas of General Surgery; Atlas of Operative Dentistry; Atlas of Obstetric Technique*

Synopses:
A synopsis is usually used to provide a brief presentation of fundamental information on a given health care specialty. The subject should become the title.
Examples: *Synopsis of Cardiology; Synopsis of Gross Anatomy*

Review Books:
Review books prepare students in a health field for examinations by a licensing or accrediting authority. The title should clearly state the field and specialty in as few words as possible.
Examples: *Review of Medical Physiology; Review of Dentistry: Questions and Answers*

Books of Readings:
A book of readings brings together information from widely scattered books and periodicals. The title should embrace the broad subject area covered.
Examples: *Readings in Personality; Readings in Radical Psychiatry*

Workbooks and Laboratory Manuals:
Workbooks generally contain questions that require writing essay answers in blank spaces. Laboratory manuals consist of experiments to be performed with results recorded. In both workbooks

and laboratory manuals, the title should contain as few words as possible, identifying the subject or course covered.

Examples: *Lab Manual and Workbook for General Microbiology; Workbook for Pediatric Nurses; Laboratory Guide for Biology*

Teachers' Guides:

A teacher's guide—an aid to help the instructor use a textbook more effectively—should be titled *A Teacher's Guide for (title of book)* or some variation of these words.

Examples: *Teacher's Guide for Teaching Mental Retardates How to Read; Teacher's Study Guide on the Biology of Human Populations*

Symposiums:

The title should be the topic of the symposium.

Examples: *Symposium on the Treatment of Burns; Symposium on Tendon Surgery in the Hand*

✔ TITLING FOR APPEAL IN INTERNATIONAL MARKETS

The following are comments made at the 39th STM Marketing Seminar in 1987 by a number of distinguished international publishing executives relative to the titling of books for appeal in international markets. The Seminar was sponsored by STM, the International Group of Scientific, Technical, and Medical publishers.

"For a medical book to travel to international markets, keep the title as simple and as generic as possible. If you want to reduce this to a formula, I would say make it 'Great, Short, Simple, Sweet.'**"**

—Susan Reinhard,
Manager, Foreign Rights,
Year Book Medical Publishers Inc.

"For medical books to be acceptable in international markets, the more narrowly specialized the title, the higher the international sales are likely to be. . . . Older books sell better in foreign markets, for example, a fifth edition of an established work. For older, long-established works, stress the edition as well as the title.**"**   *—Albert E. Meier,*
Vice President and Editor-in-Chief,
W. B. Saunders Co.

"The Japanese market for STM books is highly partial to names. If your book in science, technology, or medicine is by a well-known author, or from a well-known institution, this should be emphasized equally with the title.**"**

—Jon Cunibear,
Blackwell Scientific Publications,
Oxford, U.K.

✓ TITLING PATTERNS IN PSYCHOLOGY AND THE BEHAVIORAL SCIENCES

A study of the announcements of a score of prominent publishers of books in psychology and the behavioral sciences indicates an identifiable pattern of characteristics relative to book titling.

Approximately 55 percent of all the titles in the announcement lists were compound titles, consisting of two parts separated by a colon.

What about the remaining 45 percent that were not compound titles? These seemed to fall into three categories:

1. Short titles closely related to course names.
2. Monographs on a single subject, technique, or aspect of the social sciences, such as *Psychology of the Actor*, or *Infant Behavior*.
3. Biographies or other books about prominent individuals, such as *Freud and His Followers, Alfred Adler Revisited*, and *Darwin, Marx, and Freud*.

CHAPTER 12

SCIENTIFIC AND SCHOLARLY JOURNALS

✓ TITLING A JOURNAL: SOUND ADVICE FROM THREE PROFESSIONALS

Lore Henlein, longtime publishing professional and consultant, has started more than a dozen successful scientific journals. She offers this sound advice on journal titling:

"If your title does not immediately communicate the true and full meaning of the journal, establish a subtitle which is 100 percent descriptive and defines aim or purpose and/or audience.

"Whatever you do, don't start your title with *Journal of*; you're best off if you start off with the hottest term. Try to make the key word in the journal's title the first word."

Jonas Rosenthal, former associate publisher of the Wiley Journals Division and a longtime journals publishing specialist, concurs on the importance of beginning the title with a key word, citing two primary reasons for this advice:

1. By starting your title with an action word—such as "Computing"—you make the title easy to use and remember.

2. By so doing you also make it easier to find in the various abstracting and indexing services which will enter the title into their systems alphabetically and by one or two key words.

And key words seem also to be the crux of the titling advice from another highly-regarded publishing authority, Ben Russak, who was responsible for starting more than two dozen scientific and scholarly journals, first at American Elsevier and later at Crane, Russak & Co.

Says Russak, "I always used as my guide the message I had gotten from an Australian friend. He told me 'You can put your message on a postage stamp and it will work—if it's the right message.'"

✓ TITLING A JOURNAL: ONE MORE KEY

Eugene Garfield, president of the Institute for Scientific Information, adds a further piece of advice on titling a journal: keep it simple.

"It seems to me," says Garfield, "that people are looking for very complex titles when the simplest is the best."

Garfield also warns that the journal's title alone, no matter how clear, won't establish the journal's reputation. "Your editors and authors must do that."

✓ TITLING A NEW JOURNAL FOR PROFESSIONAL PRACTITIONERS: A CASE STUDY

When business publisher Warren, Gorham & Lamont was planning the launch of a new journal for corporate controllers in the early 1980s, the proposed title was "Journal of Corporate Accounting."

Marketing management, in reviewing the title, argued that the words "Journal of" would be counterproductive, making the title sound too academic for financial executives in corporate settings.

"Why not," was the suggestion, "drop the words 'Journal of' and give it a magazine-like title: *Corporate Accounting?*"

The suggestion was followed; launched with an extensive telemarketing campaign, the journal acquired well over 10,000 subscribers in the first four months.

Lesson learned: When you're trying to sell a journal to business professionals instead of to scientists or academics, the title of your journal should not sound like a journal.

✓ CHANGING A JOURNAL'S TITLE TO REFLECT CHANGES IN FIELD: CASE HISTORY

A journal in a field undergoing rapid change must reflect that change. Such is the case with *Mapping Sciences and Remote Sensing*, a quarterly translation journal that assumed this title in 1984.

The journal had been started in 1959 as *Geodesy and Cartography*. In 1962, the journal changed its name to *Geodesy and Aerophotography*, and in 1974, the journal underwent a third name change, this time to *Geodesy, Mapping and Photogrammetry*.

With the fourth name change in 1984 to *Mapping Sciences and Remote Sensing*, its editor-in-chief, Joel Morrison of the U.S. Geological Survey, announced that the change reflected an effort to broaden the content to cover material in cartography, remote sensing, and photogrammetry, as well as geodesy.

✓ CHANGING JOURNAL'S TITLE POSES DOUBLE PROBLEM: THE SOLUTION FOUND

A scientific society in the field of cardiology had decided to cease sponsoring the journal with the single-word title *Cardiology* as its "official" publication in 1982. It had decided to transfer its sponsorship from the existing publisher (Yorke Medical Group, New York) to another (Elsevier Publishing Company, New York), who would initiate a new "official" journal under another name.

In addition to needing a new title that would identify it as the new "official" publication on thee society, it would also have to tone down emphasis on the word "Cardiology," since the field was already crowded with publications with primary emphasis on that word.

A solution was found that neatly solved both problems. The new journal was launched as *The Journal of the American College of Cardiology.*

✓ CHANGE OF TITLE WHEN JOURNALS MERGE: CASE HISTORY

Since early in 1962, the American Chemical Society had been publishing three compatible quarterly journals in the field of chemical engineering. While their combined circulation totalled 10,000, there was an approximately 3,500 subscriber base that took all three. The titles of the three were: *I & EC Fundamentals, I & EC Process Design and Development, I & EC Product Research and Development.*

In January 1987, the ACS merged the three quarterly journals into a single monthly bearing the clear, simple title: *Industrial and Engineering Chemistry Research.*

The ACS marketing staff believed the new merged monthly, with its new straightforward title, would hold its merged subscriber base and targeted 3,350 subscribers for its first year.

By the end of 1987, the newly titled journal, surprisingly, had attracted over 1,000 more subscribers than projected—more than 4,500, compared with the original 3,500 subscriber base.

✓ PREEMPTIVE TITLING TO LOCK IN A FIELD: EXAMPLES

When you are about to publish the first new journal in any business, scientific, or professional field, it is often a good idea to drop the words "Journal of" and to preempt the subject with your title. For example, with the first journal in the field of pediatrics, a title like *Pediatrics* provides umbrella-like coverage of the field. Anyone else with a competitive publication would then have to have something else.

The American Chemical Society did it with *Analytical Chemistry*. Academic Press did it with *Analytical Biochemistry*. McGraw-Hill did it with *Electronics*. Cahners Publishing Company did it with *Packaging*. Publishing Dynamics Inc. did it with *Wallcoverings*.

✓ AVOIDING LOOK-ALIKE JOURNAL TITLES IN NARROW FIELD: A CASE STUDY

When there is one basic term that identifies a field and more than one journal using that term, there is bound to be confusion. This was the case in the late 1970s when two journals began publication in the field of computed tomography.

Raven Press had already started *Journal of Computer Assisted Tomography*. When a rival publisher prepared to launch a journal in the same field at about the same time, it realized that virtually any name it chose was bound to sound the same. The problem was solved by naming its journal *CT: The Journal of Computed Tomography*.

Since CT was often used by professionals in the field to describe the medical procedure in which images are produced of a body tissue by means of computer manipulation, this was a safe move and solved a number of problems. These included:

1. The name CT was still recognizable to people in its field.
2. It would get the title into the abstracting and indexing services under CT, a readily recognizable term.
3. It eliminated up-front conflict with journals using *Computed Tomography* in their titles.

✓ ACRONYMS: BENEFITS AND EXAMPLES OF THEIR USE IN JOURNAL TITLES

A number of journal titles in crowded fields take acronyms as their titles and find the acronym a stronger identifier than the words it replaced. Here are some examples of acronym journal titles that have caught on and become part of the language within their special fields.

Title	Organization
JAMA	*Journal of the American Medical Association*
JEMS	*Journal of Emergency Medical Services*
FASEB Journal	*Federation of American Societies for Experimental Biology*
TIBS	*Trends in Microbiochemical Searches*
LC/GC	*Magazine of Liquid and Gas Chromatography*
SIAM Journal	*Society for Industrial and Applied Mathematics*

✔ USING JOURNAL TITLES TO BUILD INTERNATIONAL SUBSCRIPTIONS

Journal titles, as a rule, do not have automatic international appeal, but there is an easy way to give many of them such appeal. Search the journal's board of editors and ascertain if its membership includes individuals from countries outside the United States.

If, in fact, there are, all you need do is add the word *International* to the title and you instantly broaden the journal's subscription potential.

This is especially true in businesses and professions where practices vary widely from one country to another. Visualize, for example, the greatly broadened overseas appeal of a *Journal of Psychiatry* when its title is changed to *International Journal of Psychiatry*.

✔ USING JOURNAL TITLE TO BUILD REGIONAL APPEAL

"Journals are sometimes less successful than they should be simply through lack of care and research of a title that will maximize appeal.

"When we launched the *Sourthern Review of Public Administration*, our ambition was to establish a general journal serving all subareas within the field. However, it was felt that a title with a regional connotation was more desirable than one denoting a desire to serve a national or international audience.

"A regional title, we thought, could be marketed more effectively in our area of the United States and thus secure the required base of subscribers needed to remain viable."*

---

*Adapted from: "Marketing Small-Circulation Journals," *Scholarly Publishing* 11 (no. 2): January 1980.

These comments are from Thomas Vocino and Jack Rabin, both in the Department of Government at Auburn University in Montgomery, Alabama. At the time of writing, approximately two years after the launch of the new journal, *SRPA* had a paid circulation base of nearly 1,000 subscribers.

✓ HOW TO NAME JOURNAL IN CROWDED FIELD WITHOUT MENTIONING FIELD: CASE HISTORY

The world of chemistry has several hundred journals with variations of the word "Chemistry" in their title. Among these, there are 21 that include the words "Surface" or "Colloid".

Therefore, when the American Chemical Society, in 1985, was considering a new journal in the field of surface and colloid chemistry, the problem of being number 22 in an already crowded field posed a serious problem.

Then one of the advisory board members for the forthcoming new journal, Karol J. Mysels, proposed a solution—a main title entirely meaningful and still lacking any mention of the much-duplicated words "Chemistry," "Surface," or "Colloid."

The recognized "father" of the field of surface and colloid chemistry was Irving Langmuir, whose achievements in the field had been monumental and whose name had instantaneous international recognition. The American chemist had died in 1957 after numerous achievements, including the Nobel Prize in chemistry. Why not name it after him?

So the new ACS journal was titled *Langmuir*, a name giving it instant identification with its field and scope of coverage.

"At first," says Cynthia Smith, circulation director of ACS publications, "we were a little skeptical about acceptance, but that was soon laid to rest, as we found instant recognition by all who were exposed and no problem with being confused with the other journals."

✓ THE RISKS OF SPECIFICITY IN JOURNAL TITLING: VIEW AND COUNTERVIEW

"Journals with generic names," says Fred Landis,* "such as *Journal for Power* or the *Journal for Industry*, may retain a high subscription level even after their range of contents has been reduced over the years. Journals with . . . names such as *Journal of Applied Mechanics* or the *Journal of Heat Transfer* can also be fairly readily introduced.

"The greatest sensitivity to change in a journal name and the greatest risk for a new journal are when the name appears to be industry-specific, for example, the *Journal of Solar Engineering* or the *Journal of Energy Resource Technology*, which appeal only to a small segment of the energy-related industry.

"Overspecificity," adds Landis, "whether referring to content or reflecting narrow primary industry interest, appears to be poison for a journal name."

Landis's attitude is counterbalanced by the personal view of the author that the professional societies, in many instances, have monopolized all the generic or major areas of science and engineering and the only entrée for a small publisher wishing to establish a position as a journal publisher is to seek out a narrow or twig area, usually an evolving one, and to offer a title serving only workers, researchers, or those with a specific interest in that area—other areas of the same fields already being covered by the established journals

A case in point is the emergence of printed circuitry in the 1950s, when McGraw-Hill's *Electronics* magazine forbade its editor to include more than one article per issue on printed circuitry. As a consequence, a new journal was started just in that one narrow area—*Electronic Design*—and the publication went on to build a circulation base of more than 130,000 and make its founders (former space sales representatives for *Electronics* magazine) millionaires.

---

*Landis, a member of the Department of Mechanical Engineering at the University of Wisconsin—Milwaukee, is also chairman of the Publications Committee of the American Society of Mechanical Engineers. His views were expressed in "Transactions Publishing by a Technical Society," *Scholarly Publishing* 17 (no. 2): January 1986.

CHAPTER 13

SCIENTIFIC AND SCHOLARLY PAPERS

✓ SCIENTIFIC PAPER TITLE PREPARATION: BOB DAY'S GUIDELINES*

A *good* title for a scientific paper, says Robert Day, for 19 years the managing editor of the American Society for Microbiology, is one that adequately describes its contents in the fewest possible words.

The title of a paper, says Day, is a "label," not a sentence. Because it is not a sentence, the meaning and order of the words in the title become more important to the potential reader.

Day offers these pointers for proper titling of a scientific paper:

✦ Do not make the title overly long. Omit such waste words as "Studies on," "Investigations on," and "Observations on."

✦ Make the title useful as a label accompanying the paper itself.

✦ Limit terms in the title to words that highlight the significant content of the paper—both understandable and retrievable by such machine-indexing systems as those used by *Chemical Abstracts, Science Citation Index, Index Medicus*, and so forth.

✦ Avoid the use of abbreviations, chemical formulas, proprietary names, jargon, and unusual or outdated terminology.

Day says most editors he talked to while active as managing editor of ASM were opposed to main title-subtitle arrangements in which the series is the main title, and the subtitle represents the actual subject of the paper.

✓ SCIENTIFIC ARTICLE TITLE LENGTHS

Nature is recognized as the world's leading journal of scientific research. It is issued weekly out of London by Macmillan, with a North American edition from New York.

---

*Adapted from: "How to Prepare the Title" in *How to Write and Publish a Scientific Paper,* Third Edition, Phoenix: The Oryx Press, 1988.

In a 1975 title-length study* of 1,000 signed research papers appearing in the 1974 issues of *Nature*, the largest number of titles (134) had eight words, followed by 118 titles of ten words, and 101 titles six words long.

Another finding of the study indicated that the length of article titles in *Nature* had changed with time. Title length increased by 5 percent from 1954 to 1959, and another 5 percent from 1959 to 1964, and again from 1964 to 1974 (although by an insignificant amount).

Studies in three similar scientific journals for the same periods also showed continuous increases in the length of article titles.

The authors of the study concluded that titles in scientific journals are becoming longer and, therefore, more informative. They cite two reasons for this increase:

1. Authors are aware of more intensive research and therefore seek titles that distinguish their papers from similar ones.

2. Scientists are increasingly aware of the importance of the title as information due to the increased popularity of the KWIC [Key Word In Context] and other title-based indexes as aids in keeping up with the literature.

✔ SCIENTIFIC ARTICLE TITLE MORE ART THAN SCIENCE†

A study of titles describing biological articles was undertaken in the 1960s with the stated purpose of impressing on writers of scientific research articles the need to key titles to retrieval from indexing systems.

Five published articles were used for the test. Each was sent to 20 scientists in the field of the published article with the request that the recipient supply a title for the paper. None were informed of the paper's original title, author, or publishing journal.

Results: When the titles suggested by the scientists were matched with the actual titles, 53 percent of the scientists' words were found in the authors' titles, and 46 percent of the authors' words were found in the scientists' titles. Further, the average word length of the titles suggested by the scientists was six.

Two conclusions may be drawn from this study. One is that titling of scientific papers is more of an art than a science, with

---

*From: "Word Count Statistics of the Titles of Scientific Papers" by P.R. Bird and M.A. Knight, *The Information Scientist* 9 (no. 2): 1976.

†Study by Lawrence Papier, George Washington University, *ASLIB Proceedings* 15 (no. 11): November 1963.

considerable leeway for variations on how the paper can be titled. The other is that scientists favor six words as the optimum length for the title of a scientific paper.

✓ **TITLING SCIENTIFIC PAPERS: INFLUENCE OF THE KWIC INDEX**

A formula introduced in 1958, known as the KWIC index,* has had a profound effect on the way scientists have been titling their papers over the past three decades.

A study examining 300 articles in 10 journals from 1958 to 1968 found a statistically significant improvement in title informativeness.†

Scientific writers apparently were concurring with J.D. Black's 1962 advice, quoted in the article that reported the study findings, that "before long the engineer, scientist, or mathematician will realize that if his title is not descriptive enought, his paper will not be used as much as it might be."

The article reinforced this statement by saying that if the KWIC formula‡ was followed in an article title, the article had much better chances of being indexed by the various abstracting and indexing services.

✓ **TITLING SCIENTIFIC ARTICLES: GUIDELINES THAT ENABLE EASY RETRIEVAL**

The title of a scientific article or chapter, says Maeve O'Connor, should convey the main subject or message in as few words as possible to permit easy retrieval.

Since the editor of the manuscript knows more about the use of titles in information retrieval than most authors, she adds, "editors

---

* KWIC is an acronym for *key-word-in-context* permuted title index, introduced by H.P. Luhn in 1958 as a prompt, relatively inexpensive means of building a temporary bridge between the contents of the current (scientific) literature and readers awaiting completion of the more slowly prepared conventional indexes.

† *Journal of the American Society for Information Science* pp. 345–50, September–October 1970. Based on address of Jacques J. Tocatlian of Merck Sharp & Dohme Research, West Point, PA, to UNESCO in Paris, France.

‡ The KWIC formula for the informativeness of titles is based on (a) a count of all substantive words in the title; (b) a count of the number of substantive title words that match corresponding words in the abstract; and (c) a count of the number of substantive words in the title that match any of the ten "leading" terms in the paper.

should have a major say in re-titling chapters or articles where necessary. Only if authors produce good arguments to back up their preferences should they be allowed to keep the original version."

Commenting in *The Scientist as Editor* (Wiley/Pitman Medical, 1979), Ms. O'Connor says it is worth remembering that a title in the form of a question or statement has more impact and is easier to understand than a title built around an abstract noun. For example, the titles "Activities of Enzymes in Plasma should Be Measured at 37°C" and "Is Dextran 70 a Lymphocyte Mitogen?" are simple, direct, and clear, conveying the author's meaning far better than alternative forms that lack verbs.

✔ THESIS TITLE PREPARATION: GUIDELINES FOR CONTENT AND STRUCTURE*

A thesis title should accurately describe the contents. At the same time it should be kept as short as possible, usually no more than about ten words. If longer, it should be divided into two parts—a short main title, followed by a subtitle.

Rather than "A Study of the Influence of Temperature, Solvent, and Metallic Salts on the Degradation of Phenols by Yeast," a better title would be "The Degradation of Phenols by Yeast: Influence of Temperature, Solvent, and Metallic Salts."

The title should be a brief summary of the document; qualifying details can be relegated to a subtitle. While a working title may be assigned at the time the project is undertaken, it is best to postpone a definitive title until the thesis has reached an advanced stage—often the work's final focus turns out to be different from that originally anticipated, especially where much previous effort has concentrated on laboratory problems of specific experiments rather than on the significance of the results.

✔ TITLING A THESIS: IMPRESSIONS OF A NOTED SCHOLAR†

Sir Clifford Allbutt, professor of physics at Cambridge University during the early years of this century, gives this advice on titling a thesis:

---

*Adapted from: *The Art of Scientific Writing* by H.F. Ebel, C. Bliefert, and W.E. Russey, New York: VCH Publishers, 1987. Used with the permission of the publisher.
†From: *Notes on the Composition of Scientific Papers* by T. Clifford Allbutt, London: Keynes Press, 1984.

"First impressions are strong impressions; a title ought therefore to be well studied, and to give, so far as its limits permit, a definite and concise indication of what is to come."

Professor Allbutt goes on to describe his personal reactions to different types of thesis titles: "From the title sent up for approval I may be able to form some notion of the composition which will follow.

✦ A concise and pointed title indicates similar virtues in the essay.

✦ A weak or diffuse title, a loose and vague argument.

"Or a title may be concise enough, yet not to the point—for example, a candidate may offer 'Three cases of pernicious anemia', a title that suggests no more than a report of the notes of three cases, whereas the writer is probably aware that a mere collection of cases, in any number, without comparison and argument, is unacceptable.

"Many titles again which give the indications of the argument well enough are wider than is necessary to denote the subject; or too abstract; or too heavily loaded with technical terms."

CHAPTER 14

SOME LEGAL AND REGULATORY ASPECTS

✓ **WHEN ONE PUBLISHER'S TITLE IS ABUSED BY ANOTHER: LEGAL RECOURSE AVAILABLE***

"The title of a book is not included in its copyright. As far as copyright is concerned, anyone can use the title for another book or any other type of work. But if the second publisher uses a title that has become associated in the public mind with the previous work, he may come up against the law of unfair competition, and the first publisher may recover damages. The second publisher may be unfairly trading on the reputation, good will, and advertising investment of the first."

So explain attorneys Harriet F. Pilpel and Nanette Dembitz, writing on the subject "The Publisher and the Law" in *What Happens in Book Publishing*.

"A publisher has one possible source of [copyright] protection when all else fails. That is the protection the courts afford against 'unfair competition.' 'Unfair competition' is a loose and flexible principle of law under which the courts try to remedy situations that offend current business mores and ethics when one businessman in publishing, or any business, seems to be unfairly profiting from or exploiting his competitor's investment or work, or in some other way unfairly undercutting him.

"The law of 'unfair competition' may protect a publisher when the law of copyright does not."

✓ **BOOK CANNOT BE REGISTERED AS TRADEMARK—BUT SERIES TITLE CAN**

The author of a juvenile title, denied registration of his creative work, went through various appeals and lost. One view of the failed

---

*Adapted from: "The Publisher and the Law" by Harriet F. Pilpel and Nanette Dembitz in *What Happens in Book Publishing*, Second Edition, edited by Chandler B. Grannis, New York: Columbia University Press, 1967. Used with the permission of the publisher.

effort, from the assistant commissioner of patents, stated that "The name is only the name by which an article of merchandise may be identified—whether a book or any other—and is not a trademark and is therefore not registrable. Since the subject matter of this registration is the name and only the name by which copies of the applicant's book can be identified, it is not a trademark and it's not registrable."

While the title of a book *cannot* be registered as a trademark, a majority ruling of the United States Courts of Customs and Patent Appeals has conceded that the name of a *series* of books can be registered as a trademark, saying "The name for a series, at least while it is still being published, has a trademark function in indicating that each book of the series comes from the same source as the others. The name of the series is not descriptive of any one book and each book has its individual name or title."

✓ **COURT ATTITUDE ON MEASURING UNFAIR COMPETITION FOR BOOK TITLES**

While book titles do not enjoy trademark protection, they often win protection from the courts through suits based on unfair competition (as mentioned in the first section of this chapter). Not all such suits are won, however. What is the criterion as to whether one title poses unfair competition to another?

Harriet Pilpel and Theodora Zavin, in *Rights and Writers*,* state their anticipation "that the test of unfair competition will increasingly be, not the test of 'palming off,' but the test of whether the defendant is, in the words of one Federal court, trying to 'earn his bread by the sweat of someone else's brow.'"

✓ **DISTINCTIVENESS IN BOOK TITLING AS A LEGAL SAFEGUARD**

If you give a literary work a title that is truly distinctive, it is often easier to show its association in the public mind with your work in the event of litigation involving unfair competition (see previous section).

While a title is not protected by copyrighting the work, as we have seen, it can be protected if it can be shown that by its use elsewhere the public is likely to be fooled into thinking there is a relationship with the original, or that it represents an appropriation of

---

**Rights and Writers: A Handbook of Literary and Entertainment Law* by Harriet F. Pilpel and Theodora S. Zavin, New York: E.P. Dutton & Co., Inc., 1960.

someone else's work, or that it will damage the name or reputation of the owner of the original work. For example, Cameron & Company, Inc., a San Francisco publisher specializing in large-format aerial photo books, had for years been publishing a series of books featuring "Above" in their titles in its specialized and readily recognizable format. The series included such titles as *Above Hawaii, Above Los Angeles, Above London, Above Paris,* and *Above San Francisco.*

When Chronicle Books, another San Francisco publisher, in 1987 issued *Above the Holy Land* in the same format as Cameron's *Above* books, Cameron brought suit against Chronicle for trademark infringement and unfair competition.

In October 1987, a Federal judge issued an injunction against Chronicle calling for both a change of title and dust jacket and requiring Chronicle to notify booksellers and reviewers of the name change.

Chronicle changed the name of its book from *Above the Holy Land* to *The Holy Land: Israel from the Air.*

✓ TITLING SAME-SUBJECT BOOKS WITH DIFFERENT PUBLISHERS: AVOIDING LEGAL PROBLEMS*

Book titling could pose legal problems for a published author who writes a second book in his or her specialized area for a different publisher. Most publishing contracts require that the author neither write nor publish a work that interferes with or injures the sale of the original work.

"Generally," says Dan Fischel, an independent publishing consultant and former head of a number of major sci-tech and professional publishing houses, "the key is whether the new work could reasonably hurt the sales of the old one (e.g., a revised edition of the earlier work).

"But," adds Fischel, "if you work in a field where your book was on one branch or level, and you do a new book in another aspect of the same field, or at an advanced level, you would not violate your agreement if your text covers new ground."

Fischel cautions, "Avoid using a title that might be confused with the first one. Customers and even booksellers tend to remember titles inexactly, and similar titles could become entangled with one another."

---

*Adapted from: *A Practical Guide to Writing and Publishing Professional Books* by Daniel N. Fischel, New York: Van Nostrand Reinhold, 1984. Used with the permission of the author.

If you sense any prospect of confusion between your new title and the former one, Fischel suggests you ask your former publisher for a written release. "It should not be withheld unreasonably," Fischel says.

✓ LEGAL IMPLICATIONS OF PROMISING TOO MUCH IN A TITLE

If you're about to title a food fad book, think twice about what you should promise in the title. Titles can kill, as this example from a report in *US News and World Report* (February 15, 1988) indicates.

The original edition of a book by the late Adele Davis was titled *Let's Have Healthy Children*, a title catering to the dream of every parent. The book recommended 3 grams of potassium chloride a day as a treatment for colicky babies.

When a Florida mother followed the book's advice, her infant son died of potassium intoxication. The publisher was hit for a large out-of-court settlement.

CHAPTER 15

AUTHOR ATTITUDES AND CONSIDERATIONS

✔ EFFECTING A TITLE CHANGE: ADVICE FROM AN EDITOR

"Some manuscripts start out with titles everyone likes," says Elsie Myers Stainton, retired managing editor for Cornell University Press.* "Some have titles the author himself questions. Some have titles the author loves and we can't stand.

"In evaluating the appropriateness of a title the editor asks, of course, whether it describes the book. Another important question is whether the title will help sell the book. The two concerns may not coincide. Here the advice of the sales and advertising departments bring us into the world of business, where producing a good book is not enough; the book must be advertised and its publishing costs retrieved from sales.

"The mention of increased sales may help you to persuade some authors, but others may not be influenced by the possibility of wider distribution. Caution: do not press an author to hurry over changing a title that he has lived with for a long time."

✔ QUESTIONABLE TITLES: THE SPECIAL PROBLEM OF SMALL PRESSES

"Making an author reconfigure a book's title—especially for a small press—is very difficult," according to Michael Coffey, former editor-in-chief of *Small Press* magazine, former editor-in-chief at Station Hill Press, and currently managing editor of *Publishers Weekly*. "It's particularly difficult for small presses because they try to service their authors to a much greater degree than the larger presses do.

"Usually, what the author wants is for the book to do well and for people to read it. Yet that same author may insist on a title that will be detrimental to those desires. I can recall a number of cases where we felt that book sales were hampered by yielding to the author's wishes on keeping the original title. Titling is really part of marketing,

---

*In *Scholarly Publishing* 8 (no. 2): January 1977.

and marketing concerns should be considered when deciding on the title under which the book will appear."

✓ WEAK OR INEFFECTIVE TITLES: DEALING WITH AUTHOR SENSITIVITIES*

Most authors of sci-tech and professional books have undergone a long and arduous struggle to complete the manuscript, and usually they view the title as part of that struggle.

The publisher should, out of respect for author sensitivity, submit proposals to the author for an alternate or stronger title as *suggestions*, based on the theme of improving the book's marketability and with no implied criticism for the author's existing title.

From this writer's own experience of more than a decade as a sci-tech book marketer, most authors will not be offended by suggestions accompanying a publisher request for a title change. Some may accept one of those proposed without question; others may prefer to select portions from two or more of the suggested changes and reconstruct a new title of their own; still others will construct a totally new title.

Where an author is firm against any change of title, often there will be no objection to appending a more meaningful subtitle to the author's original.

✓ OVERCOMING AUTHOR'S TITLE-CHANGE OBSTINACY: ONE EDITOR'S FORMULA

What does an editor do when faced with an author who has given his or her book an obviously bad title and refuses the sponsoring editor's suggestions for a change?

An editor at Macmillan Company reported he had encountered this problem on a number of occasions and had developed a useful formula for winning the author's cooperation.

"I study the author's preface, he said, "and, invariably, I find a grouping of words—the author's own—which explain the purpose or intent of the book simply and clearly.

"I then confront the author with this word grouping as a suggested title, making it clear that the suggested changes are the author's own words from the preface. It eliminates all arguments."

---

*Adapted from: "The Book Title: An Effective Selling Tool" in *Book Marketing Handbook: Tips and Techniques,* Volume 1, by Nat Bodian, New York: R.R. Bowker Co., 1980.

✓ AUTHOR ATTITUDES TOWARD NAMING NEW WORKS IN PROGRESS: STUDY RESULT

How do bestselling authors feel about disclosing the titles of books they are working on or planning? A fairly good idea can be obtained from *Publishers Weekly*, which in the first issue of every year, conducts a roundup of ten topselling authors and their plans. Examination of the ten authors in the January 7, 1987, issue produced some interesting, though not untypical, reactions.

Virtually all ten had a work in progress or were planning to start work on one shortly, and eight of the ten provided *PW* writer Beth Levine with a title or probable title for their forthcoming effort.

Only one, Chuck Yeager, author of *Yeager* (Bantam), said he was working on a book, as yet untitled, and that he expected to leave the job of titling to his editor: "Ian Ballantine will edit it and most likely name it as well."

Another, Lewis Grizzard, said he had a book in mind "but I don't have any earthly idea of what it's about. Sometime between now and March 1, I'll come up with something . . . . generally I think of the title first and then write the book to fit."* Grizzard is author of *My Daddy Was a Pistol and I'm a Son of a Gun* (Villard Books).

Three of the ten were planning four new books. Three were in the planning stage and untitled. A fourth was titled but not yet started.

✓ AVOIDING WORD DUELS BETWEEN EDITORS AND AUTHORS

"Sometimes," says Harry Neil, a successful author, "I submit six or eight suggested titles with my book outline, hoping that one will appeal to the publisher. One title I suggested as *Electronics and You* was subsequently published as *Your Career in Electronics*."

Neil's advice to first-time authors: "Before you start to type your manuscript in final form . . . make sure your chapter headings and book title are as catchy and informative as you can make them."

In his 1964 book *Nonfiction from Idea to Published Book*, Neil adds, "Titles may occasionally lead to word duels between editors and authors . . . . A tantalizing book or chapter title can make a reader want to find out what follows it . . . . In certain kinds of reference

---

*What Grizzard ultimately came up with, published in the fall of 1987 by Villard Books, Inc., was a book titled *When My Love Returns from the Ladies Room Will I Be Too Old to Care?*

books, however, it may be preferable to play it straight and use headings that explain it in the fewest possible words."

✓ AUTHOR SLIPS IN OVERLONG SUBTITLE, BUT PUBLISHER OMITS IT IN CATALOG

Edgar Palmer's introductory text to random graph theory, a 1985 volume in the Wiley series, Discrete Mathematics, is a classic example—to an extreme—of the combination of a very short front with a very long back in a compound title. The front portion is two words long, the back portion, 110 words. It is, in reality, two long sentences. The title of the text, as it appears on the book's title page, on 20 lines, is:

GRAPHICAL EVOLUTION
an introduction to the theory of random graphs, wherein the most relevant
PROBABILITY MODELS
for graphs are described together with certain
THRESHOLD FUNCTIONS
which facilitate the careful study of the structure of a graph as it grows and specifically reveal the mysterious circumstances surrounding the abrupt appearance of the
UNIQUE GIANT COMPONENT
which systematically absorbs its neighbors, devouring the larger first and ruthlessly continuing until the last
ISOLATED VERTICES
have been swallowed up, whereupon the Giant is suddenly brought under control by a
SPANNING CYCLE
The text is laced with challenging
EXERCISES
especially designed to instruct, and is accompanied by an
APPENDIX
stuffed with useful formulas that everyone should know.

The author teaches in the department of mathematics at Michigan State University. When his publisher listed the title in the large general catalog, it carried only two words: *Graphical Evolution*. The subtitle was even too long for the publisher!

✓ ORIGINS OF A BESTSELLING TITLE

The title *Future Shock* first appeared in July 1970 and went on to sell over 7 million copies in more than 50 countries, with translations in over 40 languages.

Author Alvin Toffler explains how his title was born: "In 1965, I was invited by *Horizon* magazine to write an article about our unreadiness for the future. In preparation, I began reading about 'culture shock'—the dislocation travelers experience when suddenly plunged into an alien culture. An analogy occurred to me: if people could be, so to speak, dislocated in space, why not in time? If accelerating techno-social change was creating an alien society in our very midst, perhaps much of the widespread disorientation, alienation, psychological stress, and even breakdown we see is the result of adaptational failure. Perhaps people could suffer from 'the premature arrival of the future' and go into 'future shock.'

"This analogy started me and my wife on five years of research [and the book] *Future Shock* appeared in July 1970."*

---

*From: *Current Contents*, November 8, 1982, Philadelphia: Institute for Scientific Information.

CHAPTER 16

PUBLISHER TITLING: SURVEY OF PRACTICES, POLICIES, AND PROCEDURES

✓ WATSON-GUPTILL PUBLICATIONS: BOOK TITLING POLICIES AND PRACTICES

"At Watson-Guptill," says an editor, "we start with the author's suggested title or working title; this goes into our computer system until we are nearly ready to design the jacket and prepare advertising and catalog material, when a decision is made on the final title.

"At this point, we hold a meeting—editor, editorial director, and publisher—and go through a number of titles (sometimes two, four—even six), looking at each from the viewpoint 'How will it sell?'

"We look for certain key words like 'techniques' or 'guide to.' Bear in mind our four imprints are all very specialized. One is for design professionals; one is for photographers; one is on art instruction; and the fourth is for the amusement field (we also publish *Billboard* magazine).

"For many of our books, we have evolved a successful titling formula that has worked very well for many of our specialized titles. Under the formula, the title would be *(Blank) Techniques for the (Blank) Professional.*

"Let's say you have a book for small design operations, on how they can improve their business operations. Under the formula, the title would come out *Business Management Techniques for the Small Design Office.*

"We also try for short titles, perhaps two or three words, and put most of the meaning into the subtitle to make absolutely sure there is no confusion about what the book is about. Essentially, we aim at professional audiences, and we must be very clear on how the title will look to the professional to whom it is being offered."

✓ TITLING POLICY TIED TO TELEMARKETING

There are certain publishers of business books and publications whose primary selling vehicle is the telephone. They maintain batteries of in-house telemarketing sales persons and, not infrequently, also rely on outside professional services.

For these types of publishing establishments, book titling takes on a very special if not critical significance. The people being called, when they pick up the phone, must get an immediate "fix" on what the book is about if the call is to succeed.

As one loose-leaf business publisher put it, "We don't want to intrigue our prospects; we want to inform them."

"We do this as a stated company policy by putting key words up front in the titles of our books, with the modifier at the end of the titles.

"For example, we'll title a book *Real Estate Handbook* rather than follow most other publishers, who would be likely to say *Handbook of Real Estate*. You get the action in your book title up front because it defines the market, and it's important that you let the person getting the call know immediately the subject of the call.

"Also, by doing this, you are able to ensure that your titles, when they appear in listings of books, get into the right place. We try to avoid the usual blotzy type of business title and make our titles very explicit."

✓ COMPLEX TITLE PROBLEM MADE SIMPLE: A McGRAW-HILL CASE HISTORY

One of the great book titling stories they tell at McGraw-Hill involves one of their bestselling medical books, a clinical reference used as a veritable "bible" by cardiologists all over the world.

The book was assembled by John Willis Hurst, a world-renowned cardiologist at the Emory University School of Medicine in Atlanta.

At McGraw-Hill, there was much concern about an appropriate title for the forthcoming work. As one of those involved in the title planning recalls, among the titles under consideration were "cardiovascular this and cardiovascular that . . . things like 'Principles of' . . . or whatever . . . it was very political and very stressful."

When the dust had settled and all the arguments for a title had been presented, the final title that appeared on the cover of the first and the five succeeding editions was *The Heart*.

By the way, Dr. Hurst has piloted the internationally acclaimed text through six editions, the most recent one of 2,154 pages in 1982.

✓ SEARCH FOR A TITLE THAT WAS THERE ALL ALONG: A MACMILLAN CASE HISTORY

In 1982, Macmillan Free Press published a successful work, *Cases in Competitive Strategy*, by Harvard scholar Michael E. Porter.

When Porter wrote and submitted a second, related work to the Free Press, there was great concern over an appropriate title that would give Dr. Porter's new book the right thrust. As one Macmillan marketer recalls, "All the marketing people kept coming up with different suggestions for the title. We discussed and we argued. We got several editors involved as well, but to no avail.

"Then, after several weeks with at least six of us involved, we mentioned our problem to a staff member who had not been involved previously. He looked at the author's original subtitle and said, "Look no further—just take these two key words out of the subtitle and you have your title." The two key words he suggested were "Competitive" and "Advantage." And that is what the main title of the book became: "Competitive Advantage."

Published in 1985 as a successor volume to Dr. Porter's *Cases in Competitive Strategy*, the book bore the final title *Competitive Advantage: Creating and Sustaining Superior Performance* and went on to enjoy an equal measure of success.

✓ PLENUM PUBLISHING CORPORATION: MEDICAL BOOK TITLING PROCEDURE

"At Plenum Medical Books, we generally try to go with the title submitted with the manuscript. However, many of our authors are more used to writing journal articles than books, and their book titles sometimes run too long."

The comment is from Janice Stern, senior medical editor of Plenum. Adds Stern, "When this is the case, we suggest a short title up front and try to use the author's longer version as the subtitle.

"As a general rule, about one-third of the original titles submitted with medical manuscripts are altered by the time they reach publication."

✓ TITLING ARGUMENTS DOMINATE "LAUNCH" MEETINGS OF BUSINESS BOOK PUBLISHER

At a key Manhattan trade house that specializes in business books, the head of public relations is describing a typical 'launch' meeting for a forthcoming trade business book.

"We are invited to sit in at 'launch' meetings for all forthcoming business trade books. We have a good mix of people at these meetings. Besides public relations there is the sponsoring editor and his product-line marketing staff, key people from trade sales, the head of direct response marketing, and the artist who will be responsible for or who will supervise the design of the book's jacket.

"Most of the time is spent arguing about a good title. We usually go with the best suggestion, no matter who it comes from."

✓ TITLING PRACTICES OF RELIGIOUS BOOK PUBLISHER: A SERVANT PUBLICATIONS CASE HISTORY

Titling of religious books at Servant Publications, a religious publishing house, is usually done by a meeting of marketing, editorial, and design staff. Sometimes each participant is given a chapter or segment of the book to read prior to the titling session, which is led by the editorial director or publisher.

The editor of the book starts the ball rolling by throwing out ideas. "On one book," says publicist Barbara Kolbe, "we went through about 100 suggested titles before we finally came up with the right one.

"The author had suggested *The Challenge to Take the Land: A Biblical Strategy for Christian Conquest.* But we felt that the title should be more personalized—have more meaning for the potential reader.

"We finally came up with *Courageous Living: How to Move in the Power of God's Unfolding Plan for His People.*"

At the time of this writing, the book had been out only several months, but was selling well.

✓ PRINCETON UNIVERSITY PRESS: RETITLING PAPERBACKS AND REPRINTS*

"At Princeton," says Loren Hoekzema, "we are concerned about the title's accuracy in depicting the nature of the book. Sometimes, when we are acquiring a book from another publisher, or when we are reissuing one from our own backlist, we might. . .alter the title to reflect our own press's feelings about the current market."

Hoekzema cites as an example a book published nearly 20 years earlier with an unwieldy 15-word title. It had sold about 1,000 copies and gone out of print. When it was realized that the subject was of interest to a contemporary audience trying to make connections between Western culture and Oriental mysticism, Princeton reissued it in paperback, retitling it *The Tao of Architecture*. It became a minor cult classic, outselling the earlier edition in its first four months and going through a number of reprintings.

For a book acquired from Basic Books that had originally been titled *From Private Vice to Public Virtue*, the former title became the new edition's subtitle: *The History of the Birth Control Movement in America: From Private Vice to Public Virtue*.

When Princeton staff members raised questions about whether the title change might be considered deceptive by booksellers or buyers of the earlier hardcover edition, the Press decided to include the original name on the book's cover, in advertising, and on the copyright page.

Another title change involved a 1980s reissue in paperback of a book from the Press's backlist. *The Unmaking of a President* had first been published in 1972, three years after Lyndon Johnson left the presidency. The Press reasoned that since three other presidents had been "unmade" since the book's original publication, a better title was in order. Hence the book became *Lyndon Johnson and Vietnam*.

"Title changes," observes Hoekzema, "should be done carefully. . . . They are marketing tools and name recognition is important, especially [if you] expect the earlier hardcover publicity to help the sales of the paper. A title change is a danger when the original title is so well known and has sold so many copies that the title itself becomes its own advertisement."

---

*Adapted from: "Repackaging Scholarly Books," *Scholarly Publishing* 15 (no. 3): April 1984.

✓ TITLING POLICY OF WORLD'S LARGEST PUBLISHER OF CONFERENCE PROCEEDINGS

The 300,000-member IEEE (Institute of Electrical and Electronic Engineers) is unquestionably the world's largest producer of conference proceedings, with a yearly output of more than 200 such publications.

Conference titling policy, according to Ted Gerlach, manager of conference services, is twofold. If the conference is sponsored solely by the IEEE, the title starts with the *year*, then *IEEE*, then *name of conference*, thus *1988 IEEE Conference on Office Automation.*

If, on the other hand, the conference is sponsored by the IEEE in conjunction with other outside organizations, then the title will always start with the *year* and then the *name of the conference*, thus *1988 Conference on Office Automation.*

Gerlach explained that at one time each division had a different titling policy and there was little uniformity. However, the various titling policies were unified into the existing one, which has been found acceptable to all.

✓ TITLING POLICY OF A LEADING UNIVERSITY PRESS

"At our press," says the marketing manager of a leading Eastern university press, "every title comes to me for approval." He is talking about his press's book titling policy, and continues:

"What I try to do in essence is to make sure that the title for each book we publish is as descriptive of the book's content as possible.

"This occasionally poses difficulties for use. We have some authors who want their book titles to be more imaginative than just a description. When possible, we try to reach an amicable arrangement.

"We start thinking about the book title right after the manuscript has been approved for publication. The book is presented by the sponsoring editor at a meeting of editorial and marketing people. We all kick ideas around until we come up with something we consider an improvement—if one is warranted. We go to great pains to ensure that it is something the author will agree to, but, ultimately, as marketing director, I have final say on the title."

✓ COLUMBIA UNIVERSITY PRESS: BOOK TITLING OUTLOOK

"As a university press, up until now we've had no hard and fast policy on scholarly book titling. However, as we get more and more into general-interest publishing, we're at a point where we're going to have to be more organized on this subject."

The speaker is Ann Zeller, marketing director at Columbia University Press. She continues: "Up until now, selection of a title has been a consensus between marketing, editor, and the director. More often than not, we are inclined to go along with what the author wants, so long as the sponsoring editor agrees with it.

"In the past, lacking a hard and firm policy on book titling, sometimes we'd go round and round in circles with lots of disagreement from all concerned. But more recently, we've been having meetings just on titling and this is fast becoming an area—particularly as applied to trade titles—where we're trying to be more structured in our approach."

CHAPTER 17

MARKETING AND PROMOTION: USING THE TITLE AS A VITAL TOOL

✓ THE IMPORTANCE OF TITLES IN ADVERTISING

Business and professional publications periodically conduct readership studies to ascertain the degree to which advertising is noted, read, and used. Examination by the author of many of these studies over a score of years has produced a single interesting finding: Book advertisements geared to readership interests enjoy at least twice the readership of all the other types of advertising in the same publication!

The seasoned professionals who prepare such book advertising, as a rule, are aware of this phenomenon; when preparing multibook advertisements they place great stress on book titles, often setting them in large boldface or semiboldface type, while reverting to much smaller normal or lightface type for the accompanying descriptive matter.

The logic behind this is simple: If the title appeals, the reader will continue. However, as most readers are page turners, the entire page of a multititle book advertisement may stop the reader for only a few seconds. If the scanned titles do not literally jump off the page and stop the reader's eye, the benefit of the entire advertisement may be lost.

Authors and editors should heed this phenomenon by providing books with titles that are sufficiently succinct and carry enough appeal to stop the reader and entice him or her into reading the accompanying descriptive matter.

But if the title is too long to put in print, be sure the book illustration, which carries the title, is both large and easy to read.

If you're running long in a book supplement and you have to omit the title of the book, don't refer to it as "this book." Call it something suitable, such as "this sensible guide."*

---

*If you need substitutes for the word "book," there are 68 of them in *Copywriters Handbook: A Practical Guide for Advertising and Promotion of Specialized and Scholarly Books and Journals* by Nat Bodian, Philadelphia: ISI Press, 1985.

✓ "P & R" BOOKS: CENTRALITY OF TITLE FOR MARKETING

Because information in professional and reference books tends to become outdated rapidly, the marketer usually has only one chance to make a book successful. A poor or inappropriate title can seriously hamper the success of an otherwise fine book.

As a consequence, it is good practice, once a manuscript has been approved for publication, for the marketer or marketing staff to establish whether the book's title is the best possible one from a marketing standpoint.

It is common practice to make a change in a book's title only with the approval of the author. However, rarely will an author fail to act when told that the title change will improve sales and/or attract more favorable reviewer attention.

✓ "BUZZWORDS" THAT HELP SELL PROFESSIONAL BOOKS

Over 90 percent of the thousands of professional associations and societies in the U.S. have publishing programs involving books, periodicals, or newsletters. Further, there are more than 1,500 publishers of mail-order catalogs.

An increasing percentage in each of these groups routinely offer specialized, professional, or scientific books for sale in their publications both to provide service and to increase profits. One Connecticut mail-order catalog house issued a book catalog containing over 10,000 technical, professional, and business titles in 1987.

Many of these organizations with book-selling programs have indicated to their publisher-suppliers that they are interested in books with titles that incorporate "buzzwords" with special meaning for their constituency. Here are a few examples:

✦ American Society for Quality Control: titles with *Quality* in them

✦ American Society of Safety Engineers: titles with *Safety* or *Loss Control*

✦ American Conference of Industrial and Governmental Hygienists: titles with *Industrial Hygiene, Toxicology,* or *Safety*

✦ Aldrich Chemical Company (publisher of mail-order catalogs for organic chemists): titles with *Organic*

If a publisher has an ongoing relationship with such organizations, or hopes to sell books through this "special sale" channel, it therefore makes good marketing sense to incorporate the sought-after buzzwords into appropriate titles.

✓ TITLING BOOKS FOR SALES APPEAL IN SPECIALTY STORES

Many publishers, especially small presses, create books for special types of buyers who patronize specific types of specialty stores—and title them accordingly.

The specialty establishments are quick to recognize the appeal of these titles, seeing them more as merchandise than as books, and stock them as staple items, selling them year after year. Two examples are:

1. *Marine Aquarium Handbook:* This small press title, priced at $9.95, has sold well in excess of 50,000 copies, almost entirely through pet stores.
2. *With Love from My Kitchen:* Another small press title, this book is distributed by a network of gift sales representatives to gift shops and gourmet shops. They consider it a staple and constantly reorder. Sales are close to 50,000 copies.

✓ GAINING CREDIBILITY FOR SPECIALIZED TITLES WHEN ENTERING A NEW FIELD

Ortho Books, a publishing arm of the Chevron Chemical Company, is the largest seller of garden books in the United States. A large and diversified list of books on plants and gardening are known and bought by gardeners who buy Ortho products through a 35,000 dealer/distributor network.

When Ortho decided to branch out into cookbooks several years ago, it realized it had instant credibility for its garden books but none for its planned line of cookbooks.

To establish the needed credibility, Ortho obtained an endorsement from the California Culinary Academy, which had a substantial reputation in the food industry, and Ortho cookbooks were off to a successful launch.

The lesson here is that if you intend to publish titles in a specialized field where you are not known, it is best to make an advance effort to obtain an endorsement from a credible authority within that field and use it in association with your titles.

✔ RETITLING TO POSITION BOOK FOR SPECIAL MARKET: CASE HISTORY

When Houghton Mifflin started planning a revision of the 1979 edition of *The American Heritage Dictionary of the English Language*, it gave serious thought to the fact that the college market is the major market for dictionaries. Consequently, when the new edition was issued in 1982, the word "College" was added to the subtitle and the revised edition became *The American Heritage Dictionary: Second College Edition.*

✔ CONVERTING A TEXTBOOK INTO A TRADE BOOK: RETITLING SUCCESS FORMULA*

Success formula: Take a popular textbook on a business subject, give it a benefit-oriented new title, design an attractive jacket, add illustrations, and you have a new strong-selling business book.

One business book publisher has been enjoying great success by retitling and converting successful business texts into brisk bookstore and mail-order sellers. The title and jacket design are but one of a number of changes necessary for the conversion. Others include adding illustrations, rewriting opening and closing chapters for the changed audience, and omitting problems and other textbook identifiers.

✔ HOW THE MAIL-ORDER PUBLISHERS SELECT WINNING TITLES

There is a kind of publishing in which titles are scientifically selected in a way that virtually guarantees success before a book is printed. It's book publishing invented by such mass-market magazine publishers as Time-Life and Readers Digest, which do most of their selling by mail, with their subscriber base as a prime audience.

The title is usually a theme based on a widely popular subject and calls for a series of books tied to that theme that will be sent to customers one volume at a time until they cancel or the set is completed.

Usually an in-house editor comes up with the title idea or theme. Market research experts then take over and establish whether such a subject (title) offering is likely to be successful as a mail offering. If

Book Marketing Handbook, Volume 2, by Nat Bodian, New York: R.R. Bowker, 1984.

the research establishes the theme or title as popular with mail buyers, a test mail campaign is designed.

Such a campaign is invariably a luxurious color brochure, replete with sample pages and color plates from the proposed series. It is produced in a number of variations and tested for various ingredients, including different types of format, copy, pricing, response vehicles, premium offers, etc. When the most responsive approaches are ascertained, the mail campaign is launched, usually to many millions of names.

✔ TITLING CONSIDERATIONS FOR A SEQUEL TO AN ILL-TITLED ORIGINAL

If you have or are planning a sequel to or second volume in a work whose first volume suffered from a bad title or otherwise got off to a bad start, what can you do?

When we raised this question with an academic librarian, she suggested that the publisher could issue the successor volume under another name as a new work, giving no indication that it was tied to the earlier volume. Some librarians, she added, might consider this a bit underhanded, but she could think of no other alternative.

✔ THE NEED FOR RETITLING IMPORTED BOOKS

A large number of books produced in the United Kingdom and in Europe are jointly published by American publishers as co-editions.

But frequently American publishers find that such books are badly titled for the U.S. market because they lack meaning, sales appeal, or both. When possible, the American publisher may suggest a substitute title. When time does not permit this, at least a sales-oriented subtitle can often be added.

Says Warren Sullivan, founder and head for more than a decade of the Wiley Halsted Division of John Wiley & Sons, a division devoted solely to imports, "It was much easier to get a subtitle tagged on to the title because then they didn't need the author's approval. But more often than not, the author would like the subtitle and ask that it also be used on subsequent reprints of the overseas edition."

✓ BRITISH SPELLING IN TITLE IMPLIES IMPORT BOOK AND CAN HAMPER SALES

Among many librarians, scientists, and scholars, a British spelling in a title automatically stamps the book as an import and, therefore, subject to a different level of scrutiny than a book of domestic origin.

In the physical sciences, books travel between nations and continents with little difficulty. But in some other areas, there are sharp differences in professional outlook, practice, and the type and nature of research being done. Therefore, a potential buyer seeking U.S.-oriented information will shy away from a book known to be of British (or other foreign) origin.

A number of academic libraries and a few public libraries that have standing orders for automatic shipment from their suppliers of all new books published in a subject, discipline, or category will have clearly stated on their ordering profile "no import titles."

Telltale title words that stamp books as imports include: *Aluminium, Behaviour, Centre, Colour, Defence, Favourite, Ionising, Labour, Organisation,* and *Programme.*

If you're tempted to title a book with a British spelling for the American market, the use of any such anglicized words may well be counterproductive to sales.

✓ SAME BOOK, TWO TITLES, MIRROR U.S./CANADIAN DIFFERENCES: CASE HISTORY

When *Your Guide to Coping with Back Pain* was published in late 1985 by Toronto publisher McClelland and Stewart Ltd., the book took off and sold over 10,000 copies in just four months in the relatively small Canadian market.

Delighted by this strong showing for her book, Canadian author Judylaine Fine alerted her agent, who proceeded, on the basis of this early sales history, to sell the American rights to Gareth Esersky, then a senior editor at Prentice Hall Press.

But editor Esersky said the Canadian title would not do for the American market, and obtained permission to change the title of the U.S. version to something more appropriate: *Conquering Back Pain: A Comprehensive Guide.*

Coping, the American editor indicated, "is a verb that carries a somewhat stronger meaning in Canadian than American usage; it conveys more courage and more stoicism, a legacy of British understatement."

✓ MOST IMPORTANT SALE OF A BOOK'S TITLE IS TO THE SALES FORCE*

"The final selection of a title, after acceptance of a manuscript for publication, often becomes a matter of bitter argument among author, editor, salesmen, and promotion and publicity people."

So says John Farrar, chairman of the board of Farrar, Straus & Giroux—a leading publisher of fiction and nonfiction books.

"It has been my experience that a sales department seldom likes a title when it first hears it, and often not until it has become a best seller. The more original the title, the more discussion is likely to eventuate.

"I well remember that Carl Carmer's *Stars Fell on Alabama*, Hervey Allen's *Anthony Adverse*, and Carlo Levi's *Christ Stopped at Eboli* were all considered too odd by most of the salesmen, and that the argument over Samuel Leibowitz/Quentin Reynolds *Courtroom* went on for weeks.

"Sometimes the author becomes stubborn about a change. Often both editor and author must call a halt to discussion and say 'This is it!' But if a sales department really can be persuaded to like a title it is the healthiest situation. It is they who must first sell the book to the booksellers."

✓ PROBLEMS OF BOOKS WITH AMBIGUOUS TITLES: EXAMPLES

Book titles that can interpret a book's content more than one way often wind up in the wrong display section of a book department or store or on the wrong reading list. Some examples:

✦ An editor of a book titled *Concrete Mathematics* found her book displayed with other books on concrete and construction in a civil engineering store book display.

✦ Arthur Haley's bestselling *Roots* was found being featured with books on plants in the garden and plant supply department of one discount bookstore.

✦ A listing of books about grapes, grape-growing, and wine-making included the bestselling novel *Grapes of Wrath*.

---

*From: *What Happens in Book Publishing*, Second Edition, edited by Chandler B. Grannis, New York: Columbia University Press, 1967.

✓ THE BOOK TITLE IN A PRINTED PROMOTION: GUIDELINES FOR INK COLORS

A pitfall in many otherwise excellent printed book promotion pieces is that design often ignores the intent of the piece. Readability and effectiveness are diminished either by using a too-light ink color for the title or by printing it against a patterned background or illustration, where, again, it is difficult to read.

For maximum effectiveness, book titles should be prominent and in a dark color in any promotion piece, since it is the title that stops the eye and draws attention to the descriptive copy.

This is especially true for older readers, who often need glasses for reading and are sometimes offended or turned off by any obstacles to reading ease.

✓ THE BOOK TITLE IN CHILDREN'S BOOK ADVERTISING

As a rule, most children's book advertising features the book titles with author names in a smaller or lighter typeface underneath. However, a few publishers reverse this procedure by featuring the author names prominently and play down the book titles in smaller or lighter typefaces under the author names.

A good example of the practice of selling authors as titles may be seen from the Fall 1987 children's book issue of *Publishers Weekly*, where a number of ads featured author names more prominently than the book titles.

Among the publishers featuring authors over books were Orchard Books and Aladdin Books. By contrast in the same issue, Random House and Golden Books featured titles over authors.

✓ PULPIT CRITICISM OF TITLE HELPS BOOST BOOK'S SALES: CASE HISTORY*

Sylvia Tennenbaum's 1978 novel about a rabbi's wife portrays its rabbi protagonist in unflattering terms. When the book was about to be published, William Morrow publicist, Julia Knickerbocker, sent advance copies to rabbis. As expected, many rabbis were incensed enough to name the book and preach against it to their congregations,

---

*From: *Books: The Culture and Commerce of Publishing* by L. Coser, I. Kadushin, and C. Powell, New York: Basic Books, 1982.

whereupon many congregants rushed to their local bookstores to buy a copy of *The Rabbi's Wife.*

✔ BOOK TITLE FOLLOWS OWN ADVICE—AND MAKES ADVERTISING HISTORY

When St. Martin's Press launched one of its spring 1983 titles, the event made book advertising history.

The title was *Everything You Need to Go Online with the World.* What made the launch historic was the vehicle chosen. On June 13, 1983, the title became the first ever launched to a nationwide audience of personal computer owners through their home computer terminals.

The launch vehicle was the two existing computer online services, *The Source* and *CompuServe.*

Advertising was handled differently by the two "electronic utilities." At *The Source,* with 37,000 subscribers, the title was advertised by electronic mail to 2,200 *Source* subscribers listed in a *Source* directory as having an interest in computers and communications. In addition, *The Source* issued an announcement on the title to its entire subscription base as a "What's New" feature, for a week.

At *CompuServe,* with 60,000 subscribers, the message took a different electronic format. Subscribers receive information via special-subject bulletin boards. The message was sent to over 500 bulletin boards selected by the book's author as appropriate.

The historic online title launch was a joint promotion of St. Martins and B. Dalton Bookseller. The campaign also earned the title another historic "first." It was the first title ever involved in a bookseller co-op advertising plan using a computer.

CHAPTER 18

PSYCHOLOGICAL ASPECTS AND APPROACHES

✓ HOW IMPORTANT ARE TITLES IN BOOK PURCHASE DECISIONS?

Book purchasers consider the book's title "very important" or "somewhat important" in 53 percent of book purchases, according to one study result.

The study, conducted for the Book Industry Study Group in 1978, also indicated that the book's title is more important for occasional readers than for more frequent readers, as these figures indicate:

Books Read in Previous Six Months	Title Considered Very or Somewhat Important
4 to 9	50%
1 to 3	58%

This study was based on selecting a book to *buy*. In both the same 1978 study and in another under the same sponsorship in 1983, those selecting a book to *read* considered the title very or somewhat important only 47 percent of the time.

✓ PROFESSIONAL REFERENCE TITLES SHOULD FILL A PSYCHOLOGICAL NEED

One prominent direct-mail authority says the title for a professional reference book should attempt to satisfy a psychological need as well as a rational one.

It should appeal to the potential buyer's self-image. It should also suggest a sense of security—of responding to the full range of information needs that might arise.

Most handbooks that start their subtitle with *A Complete Guide to* seem designed to meet the second need. Another title that meets the criterion rather well is *More Than You Ever Wanted to Know About Mail Order Advertising*. Although it doesn't deliver, it makes a very strong promise.

✓ SELLING SELF-HELP BOOKS: A KEY TITLE ELEMENT

What about all those book titles that give you so many ways to do something better? Peter Passell gave his theory about the success of such book titles in a *New York Times* editorial (August 5, 1987), claiming the "so many ways" approach is psychological. "Publishers of self-help books," Passell says, "discovered long ago that *47 Ways to Survive in a Cruel World* sold the socks off the *One Sensible Way.* That may be," he concludes, "because numbers enhance the illusion of control, literally taking the measure of subjects that make the reader anxious."

✓ MATCHING TITLE COLOR TO TARGET GROUP PREFERENCE

What is potentially the most effective color for printing a title on a book jacket or cover?

A 1987 color study among 374 students at four colleges that was reported in the September 14, 1982, *Advertising Age*, linked the following favorite colors to personal interests/characteristics:

✦ Outdoors: *green*
✦ Self-discovery: *purple*
✦ Upstyle clothing/fashion: *red*
✦ Organized lifestyles and intellectual pursuits: *blue*
✦ Savings and avoidance of risk: *yellow*

Book Marketing Handbook, Volume 2 (R.R. Bowker, 1984) suggests these color preferences for different types of audiences:

✦ Most attention-getting color: *red,* followed by *green*
✦ Women: *red*
✦ Men: *blue*
✦ Older people: *blues* and *violets*
✦ Younger people: *reds* and *orange*

✔ CATEGORIES WHERE TITLE APPEAL TO WOMEN MAY AID SALES

Based on a Gallup Survey,* the largest proportion of gift books, romance novels, children's books, cookbooks, and popular fiction are overwhelmingly bought by women.

Consequently, it makes sense, when considering a title for a book in any of these categories, to contemplate its appeal to women.

✔ TITLING TO APPEAL TO DOMINANT DESIRES

A book title that appeals to one or more of the dominant desires of most people has a greater chance for achieving sales success. So says L. Perry Wilbur, author of a number of successful "how-to" books, including *How to Write Books That Sell* (Wiley, 1987).

Says Wilbur in *How to Write*, "Many seek their vicarious fulfillment when they select books. They can be influenced to buy a book providing [the title] appeals to . . . the following universal desires:†

- ✦ To make money
- ✦ To be praised
- ✦ To escape physical pain
- ✦ To attract the opposite sex
- ✦ To have beautiful possessions
- ✦ To save money
- ✦ To be healthy
- ✦ To be in style
- ✦ To save time
- ✦ To be like others
- ✦ To satisfy one's appetite
- ✦ To gratify curiosity
- ✦ To avoid trouble
- ✦ To be an individual
- ✦ To be popular
- ✦ To be self-confident
- ✦ To be expressive
- ✦ To have security

Publishers Weekly, May 22, 1987.

†Table reprinted by permission of John Wiley & Sons, Inc. Copyright 1987 by L. Perry Wilbur.

To protect one's reputation
To avoid criticism
To take advantage of opportunities
To avoid effort
To have more leisure time
To have prestige
✦ To be comfortable
To advance in social or business life
To have influence over others
To be more creative
To be important

The more of these universal desires your [title] promises to fulfill the better your chances are for a best-seller."

✓ TITLING TO APPEAL TO SPECIFIC AGE GROUPS

People at various stages of their lives have shifting values and shifting attitudes.* Consequently, titles will have greater success if they take into account the values and attitudes of particular life-cycle stages.

Here is a list of the "buy" concepts that work best at six stages of the life cycle:†

✦ *Books for Teens:* This is information you need in order to belong.

✦ *Books for the Twenties:* This book will tell you what your friends expect of you.

✦ *Books for the Thirties:* This book has useful information for a good, solid person like you.

Books for the Forties: This is information that the pros and experts use.

✦ *Books for the Fifties:* This is a book to judge for yourself.

✦ *Books for the Sixties-plus:* This is a book that will show you how to be more effective and economical.

Following is the very specific breakdown of needs and values by age that underlies this checklist:

---

*Adapted from: *Why They Buy: American Consumers Inside and Out* by Robert B. Settle and Pamela L. Alreck, New York: John Wiley and Sons, 1986.
† *Ibid.*

Need and Value Emphasis by Age Group*

	Twenties	Thirties	Forties	Fifties	Sixties+
Needs					
Achievement	Medium	High	Medium	High	Low
Independence	High	Low	Low	Medium	High
Exhibition	High	Low	Low	Low	Low
Recognition	Medium	High	Medium	High	Low
Dominance	Low	Medium	High	High	Medium
Affiliation	Medium	High	Medium	Medium	High
Nurturance	Low	High	High	Medium	Medium
Succorance	Low	Low	Low	Low	High
Sexuality	High	Medium	High	Medium	Medium
Stimulation	High	Low	Medium	High	Medium
Diversion	High	Medium	High	Low	Low
Novelty	High	Low	Low	Low	Low
Understanding	Medium	Medium	High	High	Medium
Consistency	Low	Medium	High	Medium	High
Security	Low	High	Medium	Low	High
Values					
Intellectual	High	Medium	Medium	Low	Low
Economic	Medium	High	High	Medium	Low
Aesthetic	Low	Medium	High	High	Medium
Social	High	High	Medium	Low	High
Political	Medium	Low	Low	High	Medium
Religious	Low	Low	Low	Medium	High
Sensitivity	Peers	Society	Authority	Self	Utility

✓ TITLING TO APPEAL TO LIFESTYLE CHARACTERISTICS OF 20–30 YEAR OLDS

Tony Wainwright, president of Bloom Cos, New York and Dallas, writing in the July 27, 1987, *Advertising Age*, sees the 20–30 age group, which he says consists of 76 million people, as falling into three primary groups, each with its own characteristics. In part, here is how they're described:

---

*Adapted from: *Why They Buy: American Consumers Inside and Out* by Robert B. Settle and Pamela L. Alreck, New York: John Wiley and Sons, 1986. Reprinted by permission of John Wiley and Sons, Inc.

✦ *Self-stylers:* This group is the most affluent and best educated. They seek understated quality and performance, not status. They are independent minded and more inclined toward travel, entertainment and self-gratification. (30 million people)

✦ *Materialists:* The youngest segment of the 20–30 group, they are less likely to have college educations or be professional managers. They are dependent minded, wanting to own the right things and be in step with the crowd; they need to impress others. (23 million people)

✦ *Nesters:* They are high-school educated, price conscious, and content with simple things; they are struggling to make do on a modest budget. (23 million people)

CHAPTER 19

THE BOOK TRADE: TITLING ATTITUDES AND OUTLOOKS

✓ "HANDLE" OR "TITLE": WHICH INFLUENCES RETAIL BOOKSELLER MOST?

A book's title may entice a book's reader, but it is often inadequate for getting the book into a bookstore. What more often gets the book into the bookstore is the book's "handle," what author Bruce Bliven (in *Book Traveller*, New York: Dodd-Mead, 1973) calls "a blunt, philistine word salesmen use to assign the book its rightful place in literature."

In *Book Traveller*, veteran commission rep George Scheer explains a typical "handle," using as an example *Home Landscaping You Can Design Yourself* by Irv Roberts. Says Scheer, "There are half a dozen do-it-yourself landscaping books. Why another? Well, the Roberts book is practical. He is an engineer in a big company and landscaping is his hobby. He doesn't waste any time . . . he gets right down to the working specifications. And there is the 'handle' I have been using—'landscaping as a professional engineer would approach the subject.'"

✓ PUBLISHER ADVERTISES TITLE AND BOOKSELLER WHO REFUSED TO ORDER IT: A PUBLISHING LEGEND

When a leading Denver bookseller turned down what the publisher regarded as a major new title, the publisher—the legendary Alfred Knopf—found a unique way to tout both the title and get even with the bookseller.

Knopf, founder of the firm bearing his name, was in his early days as a book publisher and took offense when the Denver Dry Goods Company failed to place an order for his lead title.

Knopf responded by taking a full-page advertisement in the *Denver Post* which touted the title, but which also included this statement: "Available at all fine Denver bookstores except Denver Dry Goods."

✓ BOOKSTORE MANAGER URGES: "SUBTITLE IS WHERE YOU REALLY TELL ABOUT BOOK"

"I'm a believer in subtitles," says Jim Bowman, manager of the McGraw-Hill Bookstore in New York City.

"The subtitle," adds Bowman, "is where you really tell what the book is all about. Some may consider a subtitle a nonentity. But to the person in the bookstore that looks at a book, it's a sales tool."

The McGraw-Hill Bookstore, located in New York's Rockefeller Center, is one of the country's largest scientific and reference bookstores.

✓ CHAIN BOOKBUYER TURNED OFF BY SINGLE WEAK WORD IN TITLE

The sales rep for a large publisher made her periodic call on the buyer for one of the largest book chains. Among her forthcoming titles was one relating to jobs and careers, titled *Your Career Game.*

The sales rep had expected a substantial order for this title and was surprised at the very small order received. The buyer said the publisher was hurting the book's sales potential by calling its subject matter a "game."

In good times, he said, a potential buyer might find a book about careers with the word "game" in the title acceptable. But in this period, with many people unemployed or facing the prospect of unemployment, the word "game" in the title made too light of a serious situation.

✓ THE SMALL TOWN BOOKSTORE: SPECIAL CASE, SPECIAL NEEDS

How important are book titles to a small, independent bookseller in a tiny community of 7,000 where books are mingled with a variety of other products to help the bookseller make ends meet?

We talked with Ken Lofgren, of Durango, Colorado, whose small shop sells a variety of products in addition to books, but who considers himself essentially a bookseller.

Says Lofgren, "We are a very small community. Our people are very unsophisticated. They are put off by any book title that sounds too technical. But they'll buy a book if it has a catchy title. Mind you, I said 'catchy', not 'cutesy.' Of course, besides being catchy, it also mustn't seem too high falutin'—more like the author has a sense of humor.

"What do I mean by high falutin'? Well, my customers won't go for a book with the word 'Ichthyology' in the title. But they will buy the book if the title is something like *A Fish Tale*, even if the contents of both books are the same.

"Then, too, we're located in beautiful country and we also have some tourist trade. They look for titles about our area or books that make light reading."

✓ CAMPUS MEDICAL BOOKSTORES: EXCEPTIONS THAT PROVE THE RULE

Margaret Donohoe, manager of Dolbey's Medical Bookstore on the campus of the University of Pennsylvania, tells how some students respond to cleverly-worded titles:

"Once in a while you get a cute or interesting title—even in medical areas—and it will sell well. I remember one titled *The Man that Mistook His Wife for a Hat* by a neurologist. It was good reading and has sold well in our store.

"Another interesting title that has really sold well is *Anesthesia for the Uninterested*. The title is accompanied by a picture on the cover of two people looking very bored. . . . Many medical students really aren't that interested in anesthesia, but they really must have something and the title seems to appeal to people who really don't want to read it but have to have a book on the subject.

"There's another one that sells terrifically in our store, *Neuroanatomy Made Easy*. It's a $15 paperback. But listen to this: we also have one titled *Neuroanatomy Made Ridiculously Simple*, and that one—a paperback priced at $9.95—sells even better!"

CHAPTER 20

BOOK REVIEWERS AND REVIEW EDITORS: REACTIONS TO TITLES

✓ POPULAR FICTION AND NONFICTION: DO REVIEWERS CHOOSE A BOOK BY ITS TITLE?

Are book review editors of major newspapers sensitive to the titles of books they receive for review? According to a survey by Howard Eisenberg of a dozen such editors (*Publishers Weekly*, April 10, 1987), the answer is no.

Most of the editors Eisenberg cited said that they review mainly from galleys and they are also not influenced by jacket design or jacket copy.

To varying degrees, they say they were influenced by:

✦ The author's track record/qualifications
✦ The timeliness of the book
✦ The good name and prestige of the publisher
✦ The seriousness of the treatment
✦ Quality of style
✦ Books with big dollar deals behind them

Not a single editor quoted in the Eisenberg survey made any mention of a book's title. Most go right to the pages, generally getting their impressions from the first ten.

But when we independently posed this same question to Shirley Horner, book review editor for the New Jersey section of the *New York Times*, we got a very different response:

"My gut answer is to say 'not really,' but, in fact, titles really do influence me. I think book editors have to look at titles in terms of what's appropriate for their audience. I would feel compelled to consider a book that I felt was fit for the audience I wrote for, or one that was on a timely topic that would be of interest to my audience."

✓ TITLE-LENGTH CHARACTERISTICS OF *PW* REVIEW EDITORS' FAVORITES

When *Publishers Weekly* review editors listed their choices for "The Year's Best Books" in the January 9, 1987, issue, their selections displayed some interesting length characteristics.

Among the year's best dozen books (both fiction and nonfiction) selected by *PW* senior editor Genevieve Stuttaford, 8 had compound titles with a very short main title (1 had a single-word main title, 4 had two-word main titles, and 3 three-word main titles). Of the 4 remaining titles, 2 were of two-word lengths and 2 of three-word lengths.

Among the year's 13 best fiction books, as selected by Sybil Steinberg, the average length was two and one-half words, with not a single compound title.

Among the year's six best paperbacks, selected by John Mutter, four had three words, a fourth had four words, and one was a compound title of one word in front and nine words after the colon.

The overall preference among the best books for 1986, selected by the *PW* review editors, was for very short titles, or for compound titles with very short main, or front, portions.

✓ SUBJECT AREAS REVIEWED BY LEADING BUSINESS WEEKLY

In 1982, McGraw-Hill published the first annual issue of *Business Week Almanac*, which it described as a "reference book designed specifically for the businessman and businesswoman."

The *Almanac* included an overview of business book titles that *Business Week* magazine had selected for review. Examination of the *Business Week* choices provide a strong indicator of the types of business books business weeklies like or dislike.

Here are the highlights of the *Business Week* selections:

✦ Strong attention paid to titles about specific companies and industries

✦ Strong coverage given to books on political issues

✦ Good attention to titles dealing with foreign affairs

✦ Virtually no attention to how-to-get-rich-quick titles

✓CATCHY TITLE FAILS TO FIT TEXT OR FOOL REVIEWER: CASE HISTORY

Don't try to fool a reviewer with a catchy title if it doesn't fit the text. Professor W.V. Quine of Harvard tried this when he titled his 1987 book *Quiddities: An Intermittently Philosophical Dictionary.*

But book review editor Ellen Coughlin, in the *Chronicle of Higher Education* (October 21, 1987), reported that the subtitle *An Intermittently Philosophical Dictionary* did not really describe the book. Stated Ms. Coughlin, "This is not a dictionary and is not terribly philosophical."

But there is a redeeming feature of the title. Starting with "Q," it will find a place in indexes and references or bibliographies where few other book titles are ever found.

✓TITLE IS "HOOK" FOR FIRST IMPRESSION SELECTION BY BOOK REVIEW SERVICE HEAD

The Midwest Book Review is a Wisconsin service that provides book review programming to various educational television channels in Wisconsin. It also issues a book review newsletter, *The Bookwatch*, to 3,000 public and academic libraries in the Midwest and West.

James A. Cox, editor-in-chief of Midwest Book Review, says "Titles are critically important. We get about 50 books a day in our office for review from 2,200 publishers, and it's my job to do the initial sifting among them and to supply those titles selected for review to the 36 people who review for me.

"What do I look for in book titles? Well, first, I look for titles that are in keeping with the kind of review programs I develop. For these, we segregate appropriate titles by theme.

"The book title is second only to the dust jacket for first impression selection. When I take a look at a title, that title for me is a 'hook'—it's got to stand out. It's often helpful if the title is in tandem with the cover art. An all-type title on a cover or jacket is usually less effective than one with a picture or illustration."

CHAPTER 21

TITLE CONSTRUCTION, PUNCTUATION, AND DESIGN: THE TECHNICAL END

✓ TITULAR COLONICITY: THE HALLMARK OF SCHOLARLY TITLES

"Titular colonicity" (the presence of a colon in a title), says J.T. Dillon, "is a preeminent characteristic of scholarly publication. The colon characterizes published scholarly titles but not published unscholarly titles.

"Titular colonicity is a mark of scholarly distinction. . . . The journals give preference of place to colon-bearing titles, such that the first group of articles listed is colonic and the last noncolonic."*

Dillon suggests that to achieve scholarly publication a research title should be divided by a colon into shorter and longer pre- and postcolonic clauses, the whole not to fall below a threshold of a 15- to 20-word minimum.†

✓ LIFE SCIENCES BOOKS: THE EXCEPTION TO TITULAR COLONICITY

Examination of more than 300 newly published books in the biological sciences reviewed in 1987 issues of *Quarterly Review of Biology* indicated that only 15 percent were compound titles divided by a colon. The likely reason for the relatively small percentage of compound titles is that books in the biosciences tend to be single-topic monographs that can be explained in few words, such as (from the titles examined) *The Pupil, Biology of the Algae, Cell Components,* and *Darwin's Metaphor.*

---

*From: "In Pursuit of the Colon: A Century of Scholarly Progress 1880–1980" by J.T. Dillon, *Journal of Higher Education* 53 (no.1): 1982.
†From: "The Emergence of the Colon: An Empirical Correlate of Scholarship" by J.T. Dillon, *American Psychologist* 36 (no. 8): August 1981.

✓ "COMPILATION" OR "COLLECTION": RULE FOR USE OF EACH IN SUBTITLE

Many types of edited scholarly works have a compound, colonated title with a short front part, a colon, and then, at the start of the second part, either *A Compilation of...* or *A Collection of...* Which is best to use and when?

Mary-Claire van Leunen, a technical editor at Yale University, indicates her preference in *A Handbook for Scholars* (Knopf, 1978). She favors "Compilation" when the title represents the work of several authors gathered together by an editor; she favors "Collection" when the title represents the work of a single author. She adds that there is no real difference between a compilation and a collection; she just favors the artificial distinction for the sake of convenience.

✓ CAPITALIZATION OF WORDS IN BOOK TITLES: *CHICAGO MANUAL* GUIDELINES

Titles of books usually are written with the first letter of each significant word capitalized. This includes the first and last words of the title, regardless of their importance.

Where you have a hyphenated compound or expression, *The Chicago Manual of Style*, 13th Edition, advises you follow this rule of thumb: "(1) Always capitalize the first element and (2) capitalize the second element if it is a noun or proper adjective or if it has equal force with the first element:

- ✦ Twentieth-Century Literature
- ✦ Tool-Maker
- ✦ Non-Christian
- ✦ City-State

Do not capitalize the second element if (a) it is a participle modifying the first element or (b) both elements constitute a single word."

Acronyms are always capitalized in the title, even when they are in small letters in the text.

The Chicago Manual of Style also recommends lowercase for articles (the, a, an), coordinate conjunctions (and, or, for, nor), and prepositions, regardless of length, unless the first or last word of the title or subtitle (other style manuals advise uppercase for longer prepositions, though they vary as to whether the criterion is more than three letters or more than five letters).

Articles, prepositions, and conjunctions—irrespective of length—should be capitalized when they follow a colon or a dash. Example: *Geometry: An Introduction.*

✔ CHEMICAL TITLE CONSTRUCTION GUIDELINES FROM *ACS STYLE GUIDE* *

"In titles," says the *Style Guide* of the American Chemical Society, "do not capitalize coordinating conjunctions (and, but, or, nor, yet, so) or articles (a, an, the) or prepositions."

The manual, directed to writers on chemical and other scientific topics, further advises:

✦ Do capitalize other parts of speech, regardless of the number of letters.

✦ Do capitalize the first and last words of a title . . . regardless of the part of speech, unless the word is mandated to be lower-case (e.g., pH).

✦ Do not capitalize the "r" in "X-ray" in titles.

✦ In titles with compound words, capitalize both words if the compound is a unit modifier (High-Temperature System, Base-Catalyzed Cyclization, Thyrotropin-Releasing Hormone).

✦ Capitalize each component of hyphenated words if the compound would be capitalized when standing alone.

✦ Do not capitalize abbreviated units of measure, but do capitalize spelled-out units of measure, thus: "Analysis of Milligram Amounts" *but* "Analysis of 2 mg. Amounts."

✔ MEDICAL TITLE CONSTRUCTION GUIDELINES FROM AMA *MANUAL*†

The American Medical Association, in its *Manual for Authors and Editors* (7th Edition, 1981), offers scientists a number of clear and useful instructions for construction of titles. Some of their recommendations are:

✦ The title should be concise, informative, and clear.

---

*The ACS Style Guide: A Manual for Authors and Editors edited by Janet S. Dodd, American Chemical Society, 1986.

†When it comes to titling, the AMA *Manual* itself has undergone a title change with its 7th Edition. In previous editions, it was called *Stylebook/Editorial Manual of the AMA.*

+ The title should be grammatically correct.
+ All numbers are spelled out at the beginning of a title.
+ In English-language titles, capitalize the first and last word and each word that is not an article, preposition, or conjunction.
+ Numerals in titles: spell out all numbers from one through ten.
+ A subtitle may be used to amplify the title but should not be used as a substitute for or duplication of the main title.
+ In book references, use a colon between title and subtitle.
+ In periodical references, use a colon between volume and page numbers.

✔ WHEN TO HYPHENATE OR NOT HYPHENATE IN TECHNICAL TITLES

The *Prentice-Hall Author's Guide,* based on *Webster's New World Dictionary, Second College Edition,* offers these guidelines for hyphenation.

Compounds are hyphenated:

+ When they consist of a prepositional phrase.
  Examples: "Off-Center Axis," "Into-Orbit Arc"
+ When "Self-" is the first element.
  Examples: "Self-Sealing," "Self-Starter"
+ When a vowel would be doubled.
  Examples: "Intra-Atomic," but "Intranuclear"
+ When the compound is a technical unit of measurement ending in Year, Day, Hour, Minute, Second, Mile, Foot, Inch, Pound, or Ton.
  Examples: "Light-Year," "Foot-Pound"

Terms consisting of capital letter and a noun are hyphenated only when they are used as attributive adjectives.

+ "I Beam," but "I-Beam Structure"
+ "X ray," but "X-ray Tube"

Do not use hyphen in compounds containing an adverb ending in "ly."

+ "Regularly Spaced Intervals"

✔ WHEN CREATIVE WORK MAY BE CLASSIFIED AS BOOK FOR REFERENCING PURPOSES

Since titles of books and titles of nonbook works are referenced differently insofar as punctuation is concerned, it is useful to know which types of works are classified as books and italicized, and which are classified as nonbooks and placed in quotes for referencing purposes. The table following should make all clear:*

Classify as Book if it is:	*Classify as Nonbook if it is:*
✦ A multivolume work	✦ A magazine or journal article
✦ Anything that contains articles by different people	✦ A master's thesis (unless published as a book, and then *only* the thesis that is the book)
✦ A journal	
✦ A magazine	
✦ A newspaper	✦ A long novella
✦ A conference proceeding	✦ A short story
✦ A doctoral dissertation (but not a master's thesis)	✦ A poem (unless book length and bound as a book)
✦ A musical (but not a song)	✦ A chapter of a book
✦ A record album (but not one side)	✦ A report
	✦ A sketch, print, or painting
✦ A motion picture title	✦ Title of television or radio program

✔ PLACEMENT OF TITLE ON BOOK COVER: A DESIGNER'S VIEWS

How should a book title be represented on the cover of a business, professional, or scientific book?

The question was posed to the design manager, a longtime cover design professional, at a major New York publishing establishment.

"The book's title should take priority over the graphics; it should always be the first thing seen on the cover.

"I try to avoid hyphenating any word in a book's title on a cover. If the words are very long, as is sometimes the case with medical books, I try to avoid word breaks by either using smaller-size type, by

---

*Compiled from: *A Handbook for Scholars* by Mary-Claire van Leunen, New York: Knopf, 1978 and *The Chicago Manual of Style*, 13th Edition, Chicago: University of Chicago Press, 1982.

running the title up the side, or by placing it on the cover diagonally.*

"A good rule to bear in mind for titles on book covers is that the *editorial sense* must always take priority over the *design sense*."

✓ PHYSICAL SIZE OF TITLE ON THE BOOK: PRACTICAL GUIDELINES

As an author or editor, you may be asked to initial your approval of jacket artwork or stamping proofs of a book's title as it will appear on a book's binding. You should be wary of a possible pitfall regarding the physical size of the book's title before initialing your approval.

Here's why: Occasionally, a publisher will advertise a book with accompanying illustration and omit mention of the book's title in the copy, relying entirely on its appearance in the illustration.

A pitfall of this practice is that in some advertising the book illustration may be only an inch or a little more in height. With this drastic reduction in size, the title cannot be read.

A case in point, recalled by the author, was a 2-column x 10" advertisement for a new edition of a professional directory in which all mentions in the advertisement and coupon referred only to *The Directory* without once ever giving its name. The accompanying illustration for the directory had been reduced to 1½" high, so that the size of the title was about one-third the height of normal newspaper type and not readable.

Be wary, if asked to approve a book or jacket design, to ensure that the book's title is of sufficient size so that if radically reduced in a catalog or advertising illustration it will still be readable.

Some trade publishers make titles prominent enough that if the author appears on a TV talk show with book in hand, the viewer can still clearly make out the book's title on the screen.

✓ WORDBREAKS IN TITLE ON COVER AND JACKET: GUIDELINES

Where words must be broken in a title, the best guide to follow is *Word Division*, the supplement to the U.S. Government Printing Office *Style Manual* (8th Edition, 1984). This is a minidictionary that

---

*A clear illustration of this title-design tactic is seen in the 1988 Dutton book *Revolutionaries and Functionaries: The Dual Face of Terrorism*. Each of the two words in the main title runs the full spine-length of the book jacket, starting lower left and running up at a 30-degree angle to the middle of the top. The subtitle runs at right angles. The effect is extremely eye-appealing.

follows the word breaks of the Webster dictionaries, relying mainly on *Webster's Third Unabridged*, published in 1961.

Some useful wordbreak rules from this manual that may be helpful in jacket and book cover titling include:

✦ A word should be divided according to pronunciation. It should be divided so that the part of the word left at the end of the line will suggest the whole word.

✦ Divide words of three or more syllables on a vowel when that choice is possible.

✦ Words with short prefixes should preferably divide on the prefix.

✦ If possible, prefixes and combining forms of more than one syllable are preserved intact, such as *infra, macro, multi, over, semi*, etc.

✦ Solid compounds are divided preferably between the members: *proof-reader, humming-bird*.

✦ When two adjoining vowels are sounded separately, divide between them: *cre-ation, gene-alogy*.

✓ MAKING LENGTHY TITLE LOOK SHORTER ON BOOK COVER: CASE STUDY

How do you introduce a major new consumer reference with a title seven words long and make it look like a short title?

The answer is with design—and that's exactly what McGraw-Hill did when it introduced, in late 1987, the first edition of a household drug reference, *The Family Physician's Compendium of Drug Therapy*.

To avoid giving the title a lengthy look, they ran the first three words of the title adjacent to and up the spine, to form a right angle with the last four words which ran inward from the spine, horizontal with the top of the binding (see illustration, following page).

And, so as not to scare off the bookseller readership, the announcement advertisement in *Publishers Weekly* (July 31, 1987) ran a 7½" high illustration of the book cover so that the oversized special-effect title on the cover would not have to be repeated in the text.

✓ COLOR OF TITLE ON BOOK COVER: PRACTICAL GUIDELINES

When the color of a book title is in poor contrast with the binding cloth color on an unjacketed book, it can create legibility

A Long Title Made to Look Shorter

problems when the book has to be photographed or otherwise displayed for public viewing. Poor contrast between title and binding
color can also hamper ease of location on a library shelf.

Yet the mistake of bad contrast for titles of unjacketed books is
one that is frequently repeated at many scientific publishing houses.
At one biomedical show in late 1987, we saw such poor-contrast
covers as titles in gold on brown, silver on light gray, white on beige,
and green (metallic) overprinted on green binding cloth.

At the same show, we noticed many high-contrast combinations,
such as gold or silver titling on black or charcoal gray, yellow titles on
dark blue, and orange titles over blue or green.

While ink color of printed titles on book covers is not the
province of either author or editor, where the opportunity to comment
on colors presents itself, care should be taken to ensure that color
combinations specified for title and binding offer some degree of

contrast. (For the possible psychological implications of colors for titles, see Chapter 18—but still make sure to use a contrasting binding color!)

✓ BINDING COLORS TRANSFORMED INTO BOOK TITLES: CASE HISTORY

In some fields, consumers come to rely on binding color rather than title to identify a particular book; ultimately, the book's binding color actually becomes the title.

A notable example is the series of books providing industrial electric power standards and published by the Standards Department of the IEEE (Institute of Electrical and Electronic Engineers).

When the IEEE first began publication of the various power standards volumes in 1959, the first "standard" had a red cover. It was followed shortly thereafter by another "standard" in a green cover. Soon both mail and phone orders began to identify them as the "Red Book" and the "Green Book" rather than by their lengthy technical names.

As a consequence of such identification, by 1973–74 the names of the colors were added to the book spines of the various "standards" as they were published.

And in a fall 1987 brochure, all the different standards volumes were listed on the cover by color only, and the inside carried as main titles for each standard the following: *Red Book, Green Book, Gray Book, Buff Book, Brown Book, Orange Book, Gold Book, White Book,* and *Bronze Book.*

The actual titles, in effect, have become the subtitles; the binding color has become the permanent identifier for each particular volume.

✓ BINDING COLOR GIVES BOOK ITS INFORMAL "TITLE": CASE HISTORY

Somewhat similar to the example of the IEEE standards volumes in the previous entry is the story of *Advanced Inorganic Chemistry*, a widely used text where the first two editions had an orange binding.

When the publisher, John Wiley & Sons, changed the binding color to beige for the third edition, the author protested, saying that the book was referred to by many as "The Orange Book."

Wiley heeded the author's protest and the fourth and fifth editions reverted to the earlier orange binding.

✓ COLOR COMBINED WITH EMBOSSING: NEW EMPHASIS OF MASS-MARKET TITLES

Increasingly, mass-market publishers are emphasizing already brightly colored titles, or titles in silver or gold, by embossing them to create a three-dimensional effect and give them a traffic-stopping quality.

The embossing, or raised-surface process, is one in which stamping produces a raised image above the cover. It is done after printing and before binding. Embossing is done by means of a sharp, raised metal dye in the exact shape of the title to be embossed. Heat is usually applied to the paper at the time of impression to soften the paper and prevent cracking.

This is virtually a universal trend with paperback romances. (See also Chapter 18, the section titled "Categories Where Title Appeal to Women May Aid Sales.")

✓ WHEN COVER DESIGN IS MORE IMPORTANT THAN TITLE

In at least one category of publishing—mass-market horror—cover design is more important than title. Those who publish in this field turn out a steady stream of books with rather lackluster titles and put their money and effort into the cover design.

What constitutes a successful cover design for a horror book?

Norman Lidofsky of Berkeley Publishing, a leading horror publisher, says success lies in a "creepy" cover, "the creepier the better" (*Publishers Weekly*, December 4, 1987).

"What could be hidden behind that wall, behind that closet or under the bed?"

Two additional opinions on horror cover design, both in the same *PW* article, corroborate Lidofsky. Says article author Steve Sherman, "Cover art itself often becomes the primary object of purchase." Says mass-market horror buyer David Thorson of the Waldenbooks chain, "Cover art sells the book."

CHAPTER 22

MAGAZINES, MAGAZINE ARTICLES, NEWSLETTERS, AND SOFTWARE

✓ MAGAZINE TITLING: ADAPTING TO CHANGING TIMES

Magazine titles often must change with the times. Such title changes rarely affect their circulations adversely and sometimes work to their benefit.

Title changes are usually made not in the main title, but in the subtitle. Then, after the subtitle has caught on, the main title is dropped and the subtitle retained as the main title. Some examples:

ZIP magazine: The subtitle *Target Marketing* was added, making the title *ZIP: Target Marketing*. With the August 1986 issue *ZIP* was dropped and the magazine became *Target Marketing*.

Reporter of Direct Mail Advertising: As the term "direct marketing" came into vogue in the 1950s and 1960s, it added the subtitle *The Magazine of Direct Marketing*. With the passage of time, the words *Direct Marketing* were increasingly emphasized; subsequently, the other words were dropped and the title *Direct Marketing* emerged.

Transaction: The popular social science magazine, started in the 1960s, became *Transaction: The Magazine of Modern Society* in 1971, and ultimately became just *Society*.

✓ PUBLIC INTEREST MAGAZINE TITLED TO SOUND LIKE SCIENTIFIC JOURNAL

Bulletin of the Atomic Scientists has the look and sound of a very scientific publication, and most people think of it that way. But its editor, Len Ackland, says the Chicago-based magazine is something entirely different.

"It was founded in 1945," says Ackland, "by scientists convinced that global nuclear war can be prevented only by an informed public." He describes *Bulletin of the Atomic Scientists* as a "nontechnical magazine providing an information resource and forum for debate about the arms race and related issues of the nuclear age that reaches 25,000 subscribers in 70 countries."

✓ MAGAZINE TITLE IDEA THAT HELPED SELL SPONSORSHIP: CASE HISTORY

In 1984, editor Byron Dobel, proposed to the *American Heritage* management the possibility of spinoff magazines that would concentrate on specific areas of the American past.

Dobell's proposal to his management was coupled with the idea that each spinoff be sold to a sponsor who would back the magazine the way a corporation backs a television program, getting its name associated with the publication while leaving the creative authority to others.

The first spinoff magazine would deal with invention and technology. It was backed by General Motors and published three times a year. *American Heritage of Invention and Technology* first appeared in April 1985.

For its sponsorship, GM gets a boxed statement explaining the reason for the sponsorship; advertising for various GM divisions; and complimentary distribution to 270,000 executives, engineers, scholars, teachers, government officials, and others.

American Heritage also places it on newsstands and in mid-1987 had 5,000 paid subscribers.

✓ MAGAZINE CHANGES NAME TO REFLECT EDITORIAL THRUST

For over 21 years, the magazine *Curriculum Product Review* served a universe of close to 150,000 district-level educators with information about new educational products for the K–12 market.

Beginning with the fifth issue of Volume 22 in January 1988, the magazine's name was changed to *Curriculum Product News*. Editor Howard Reed explained the change of name this way: "We dropped the *Review* in our title because we report; we don't review. Every report contains news of new products. *News* is the key word."

✔ MAGAZINE NAMES THAT PARODY OTHER SUCCESSFUL MAGAZINES: EXAMPLES AND LEGALITY

Magazine titles that parody other successful magazines are finding increasing acceptance in bookstores and providing an unusual revenue source for otherwise traditional book publishers. Here are a couple of recent examples:

✦ *Dogue*, a witty parody of *Vogue* magazine for dogs, was published in 1986, using "glamorous" dog models in sections on fashion, health, and travel.

✦ *CQ (Canine Quarterly)*, issued late 1987, was a spoof on *GQ (Gentlemen's Quarterly)*.

Are such parodies legal? Apparently yes, according to a November 14, 1987, *Wall Street Journal* report dealing with magazine titles that parody other successful magazines. The report included the statement that "US trademark laws leave room for such parodies."

✔ MAGAZINE NAME SO PRECISE IT INFRINGES ON TRADEMARK: CASE HISTORY

When a magazine was started early in 1987 devoted exclusively to Porsche cars, the publisher named it *Porsche Magazine*. But in its early months, Porsche Cars North America Inc. brought suit against the magazine, claiming infringement of trademark rights.

The magazine changed its name to *Excellence*. And in case anyone among the subscribers did not know what kind of excellence the magazine was referring to, publisher Tom Toldrian added the subtitle: *A Magazine About Porsche Cars*.

✔ MAGAZINE NAMES THAT OFFER NO CLUE AS TO CONTENT

✦ *Parabola* is a quarterly journal about myths, folktales, and spiritual traditions. The dictionary defines parabola as "a plane curve formed by the intersection of a right circular cone with a plane parallel to a generator of the cone."

✦ *Taxi* is the name of an international high-fashion magazine for women. For most of us, a taxi means a taxicab.

✦ *Cricket* is the name of a monthly magazine for children that emphasizes reading and art, nonfiction, poetry, jokes and riddles, crafts—and even recipes. For those in the know, cricket is either an insect, a metal snap toy, or a field game involving two teams of 11 players each.

✦ *Purple Cow* is, well, a purple cow. But it's also a magazine with general-interest articles for readers aged 12 to 18, stressing morality without preaching.

✦ *ZYZZYVA* is a 6″ x 9″ 136-page perfect bound literary quarterly published out of San Francisco "to assert the community of West Coast writers & Artists." Its content of fiction, nonfiction, poetry, and dramatic scripts won the magazine two literary prizes in 1987, its third year of publication. The name, *ZYZZYVA*, is not a dictionary word, but by the time many recipients of the magazine's various direct-mail promotions discover this, they are intrigued enough to read the simple, straightforward promotional copy and enter subscriptions. While it is the offbeat name, *ZYZZYVA*, that attracts the attention of subscribers, it is the offer of a full refund after the first issue if not completely satisfied that holds them.

✓ TITLING A GENERAL-INTEREST ARTICLE: SIX RULES THAT MUST BE FOLLOWED

The nonfiction book strives for a simple title indicating its content. However, articles for nonspecialist magazines have much more latitude in their titles.

"If it has a catching lilt to it," says Walter Steigleman, a journalism professor at Indiana University, "the magazine editor welcomes it. However, these rules must be followed:*

1. It must be honest.
2. It must fit the article.
3. It must show good taste.
4. It cannot appropriate another title or a copyrighted slogan or a registered trademark.
5. It must be brief.
6. It must contain words easily understood by the general reader."

---

*Adapted from: *Writing the Feature Article* by Walter A. Steigleman, New York: Macmillan, 1950.

✓ TITLING A NONFICTION ARTICLE: ADVICE OF HAYES JACOBS

It is helpful to editors, in sizing up story possibilities from queries, if you offer them a working title. Indeed, an appealing title can itself provide the lure that will attract an editor to your idea. Good titles have strong sales appeal, as well as informative value, and it is the writer's duty to offer an appealing, effective title for anything submitted for publication.

This is the advice of Hayes Jacobs,* who adds, "I've seen many excellent writers whose best titling efforts are pale, and crude. Most bad titles are the result of applying only a label to a story. A good title is not a label, but a lure."

✓ TESTING ARTICLE TITLES FOR GREATEST SALES APPEAL: CASE HISTORY

Advertising hall-of-famer John Caples was once asked by the circulation manager of *Readers Digest*, "How can we find out which articles have the greatest sales appeal to readers?"†

Caples came up with an answer that the *Digest* turned into a science for title selection. Months in advance of publication, the titles would be listed in a newspaper advertisement. Readers would be offered advance copies of preferred articles on a mail-in coupon.

After tallying the responses, the *Digest* would select the most popular titles and feature them on a sticker on that particular issue sold at news and magazine stands.

Since approximately 20 percent of *Digest* sales are made this way, this method of presenting the most appealing titles has helped produce untold millions of sales over the years.

---

*From: *A Complete Guide to Writing and Selling Non-Fiction* by Hayes Jacobs, Cincinnati: Writer's Digest Books, 1967.
†From: *How to Make Your Advertising Make Money* by John Caples, New York: Prentice Hall, 1983.

✔ TITLE GUIDELINES FOR NEWSLETTERS*

When starting a newsletter, says Howard Penn Hudson, founder and president of the Newsletter Clearinghouse, "a good name will help position your newsletter and spell out its promise, as well as reinforce your advertising."

"Choose a name that helps position your newsletter

✦ for example: *Moneysworth*
  instead of: *The Ginsberg Letter*

✦ another example: *Newsletter on Newsletters*
  instead of: *The Hudson Letter*

"Put your advertising promise in the name, again like *Moneysworth.*

"Make the name memorable, again like *Moneysworth, Moneytree,* or even *Money.*

"Choose a name that identifies the newsletter subject quickly. Don't pick a name that is so vague that it could apply to almost anything.

"Choose a name that is easy to pronounce.

"Remember that names should be descriptive. If you can't think of something both clever and descriptive, settle for something descriptive. There must be at least twenty newsletters named *Impact.*

"Impact on what, or for whom? Magazine-type names like *Life* and *Look* don't belong in newsletters. You want your prospects to know what field you are covering. . . .

"Consider the names of some of the older, established newsletters, such as *Television Digest* or *Telecommunications Reports.* The emphasis is on description, not cuteness.

"Perhaps my favorite name for a newsletter is from Business Publishers, Inc., Washington, which has a host of environmental newsletters. It is called simply *Sludge.*

"Now, that's impact!"

---

*Adapted from: *Publishing Newsletters,* Revised Edition by Howard Penn Hudson, New York: Charles Scribner's Sons, 1988. Used with permission of the author and the publisher.

✔ TITLING OF EDUCATIONAL SOFTWARE: INGREDIENTS OF AWARD WINNERS

When a contest was held to select the best in higher education software in 1987, the judges—instructional designers, software experts, and college faculty—selected winners in seven educational categories.

The average award-winning title, a factor in the selection, was simple, to the point, and averaged less than four words in length.

The winning software titles: *Introduction to General Chemistry; Mechanical Properties of Active Muscle; Standing Waves; Exploring Small Groups; Interactive Video Disc Lessons for General Chemistry; Event-Log;* and *The Would-Be Gentleman.*

CHAPTER 23

TITLING TIDBITS AND CURIOSITIES: A POTPOURRI

✔ THE MOST HEAVILY ADVERTISED TITLE IN BOOK PUBLISHING

Announcement issues of *Publishers Weekly*, the book trade journal, frequently show promotion budgets for the major new trade paperbacks. As a rule, they range from $20,000 to $50,000. Consequently, it is hard to visualize a paperback that annually receives over $2 million in retail advertising.

There is one, however: it's *The World Almanac and Book of Facts*, published in November by Pharos Books of New York City. The *Almanac* is distributed to the book trade by Ballantine Books. However, it also has over 140 major newspaper co-sponsors nationwide, each of which launches its own ad campaign for each new edition. The 1988 paper edition, with 928 pages, was priced at $5.95.

✔ "INSTANT BOOKS" THAT BECAME INSTANT BESTSELLERS

Titles that "plug" into a major news event while public interest is at its peak are called "instant books." The books, usually published by the mass-market paperback houses, take their titles from the theme of the event and enjoy a virtually instant, though very short, sales life.

One example was the Pocket Books instant paperback published during the 1987 congressional hearings on the Iran-Contra affair.

The star witness, Lieutenant Colonel Oliver North, took the witness stand for four days (July 9, 10, 13, and 14), and his testimony was televised on all the major TV networks and dominated the headlines of the nation's newspapers during that period.

Three days after North concluded his testimony, on July 17, Pocket Books issued a paper edition of North's testimony, titling it *Taking the Stand*. The 775,000 printing was an instant sell-out,* half going to bookstores, the other half to newsstands, supermarkets, and

---

*A published report in November 1987 indicated that approximately half of the "sold" copies of *Taking the Stand* were eventually credited as returns.

other retail outlets. For the week of July 19 through July 25, *Taking the Stand* was listed as the number one book among paperback nonfiction bestsellers (in the August 9, 1987, *The New York Times Book Review*).

Some other notable instant books include *Franklin Delano Roosevelt—A Memorial*, published by Pocket Books on April 18, 1945, just six days after Roosevelt's death; *Strike Zion*, the story of the Arab-Israeli War of June 1967, published by Bantam just 21 days after the war; and *The End of the Presidency*, published by Bantam four days after President Nixon left the White House in 1974.

✓ COLOR AS PART OF A BOOK TITLE

Authors frequently use color as part of a book title, as this sampling of bestsellers indicates:

✦ *The Color Purple*
✦ *A Clockwork Orange*
✦ *The Scarlet Pimpernel*
✦ *Red Storm Rising*
✦ *Yellow Dog Contract*

A classic example of the use of color in book titles may be found in the works of mystery novelist John D. MacDonald, with his numerous Travis McGee novels. He always wove a color into the title of any volume featuring his Travis McGee character. A few of many examples are:

✦ *The Girl in the Plain Brown Wrapper*
✦ *Nightmare in Pink*
✦ *One Fearful Yellow Eye*
✦ *Pale Gray for Guilt*
✦ *Dress Her in Indigo*
✦ *The Long Lavender Look*
✦ *A Tan and Sandy Silence*
✦ *The Lonely Silver Rain*

How MacDonald got his idea for naming the McGee novels after colors is a matter of speculation. Was he influenced, perhaps, by the greatest mystery writer of them all—Sir Arthur Conan Doyle—who first introduced Sherlock Holmes and Dr. Watson in the 1887 *A Study in Scarlet*?

Perhaps the greatest example of color in relation to book titles is that of Golden Press, which publishes its Little Golden Books® in various series that all bear "Golden" as part of their name.

✦ Little Golden Books
✦ Golden Friendly Books
✦ Golden Look-Look Books
✦ Golden Classics
✦ Big Little Golden Books
✦ Golden Gatefold Books
✦ Golden Super Shape Books
✦ Golden Junior Classics
✦ Golden Books for Beginners

The "Golden" trademarks are the property of Western Publishing Company.

✔ USING AUTHOR'S "COLOR" NAME TO HELP SHAPE BOOK TITLE

There are occasions when publishers capitalize on an author with a color in his or her name to help shape the author's book title.

Rabbi Lionel Blue's "Thought for the Day" is a popular radio feature in the United Kingdom. When Hoddard & Stoughton published a volume of Rabbi Blue's thought-provoking humor in 1986, they titled it *Blue Heaven.*

When, in the fall of 1987, H&S published a second volume of stories based on Rabbi Blue's experiences, they titled it *Bolts from the Blue.*

When Victor Gollancz Ltd., published the rabbi's cookbook, which blended anecdotes, humor, and theology with recipes, they titled it *Kitchen Blues.*

And finally there is Burt Greene, who is a food columnist in the *New York Daily News* and the *Los Angeles Times.* When in 1984 E.P. Dutton published a book with 500 of Greene's recipes for vegetarian and nonvegetarian dishes, they titled it *Greene on Greens.*

✔ BOOK TITLES BUILT AROUND DAYS OF THE WEEK

Mystery writer Harry Kemelman introduced his "detective" character, Rabbi David Small, in *Friday the Rabbi Slept Late.* The book was a considerable success, and subsequent titles in the series continued to use the day-of-the-week title formula, making it easy for readers and reviewers to remember his titles—and look for more.

Rabbi Small subsequently appeared in *Saturday the Rabbi Went Hungry, Sunday the Rabbi Stayed Home, Monday the Rabbi Took Off, Tuesday the Rabbi Saw Red, Wednesday the Rabbi Got Wet,* and *Thursday the Rabbi Walked Out.*

Although the days of the week exhausted themselves, Rabbi Small hadn't. Kemelman has retained a temporal element in his subsequent titles with *Someday the Rabbi Will Leave,* and the more recent (1987) mystery adventure *One Fine Day the Rabbi Bought a Cross.*

Many authors like to start their book titles with a day of the week, if a study of the 1987–88 edition of *Books in Print* is any indication. Sunday is the overwhelming favorite with 69 title starts, followed by Saturday with 53, Monday with 25, Thursday with 18, Friday with 15, and Tuesday and Wednesday with 5 each.

✔ HUMOROUS TITLE AIMS AT PSYCHOLOGISTS/PSYCHIATRISTS—AND SUCCEEDS!

The title is weird—and the book's contents even weirder. They're the creation of New York psychologist Glenn C. Ellenbogen. The book is an anthology of entries from a quarterly journal created and edited by Ellenbogen that pokes fun at mental health professionals and affords them an opportunity to see humor in their work. The book's title: *Oral Sadism and the Vegetarian Personality.*

Do psychiatrists and psychologists think it is funny? Ask Brunner/Mazel, the book's publisher. Brunner/Mazel, Inc. enjoys a worldwide reputation as a publisher of professional books on psychoanalysis, psychiatry, psychology, and related fields, and as the largest mail-order bookseller and distributor in these fields for related books of all publishers.

Oral Sadism, the first humorous book issued by Bruner/Mazel in the 46 years since its founding, was their topselling title for nearly a year after its publication.

At the 1986 Frankfurt Book Fair, where author/editor Ellenbogen showed *Oral Sadism,* it won the Diagram Group Prize for the most improbable title offered at the Fair.

Oral Sadism, though, is no more offbeat a title than the publication from which the entries are drawn: *Journal of Polymorphous Perversity.*

✔ BIZARRE BOOK TITLES THAT WON AWARDS FOR THEIR ZANINESS*

The Diagram Group Prize, noted in the preceding entry, was created in the 1970s to enliven the proceedings at the Frankfurt Book Fair, an annual event in Frankfurt, West Germany, at which thousands of publishers gather mainly for the purpose of contracting sales rights.

Recent winning titles include:

✦ 1985: *Natural Bust Enlargement with Total Mind Power: How to Use the Other 90 Per Cent of Your Mind to Increase the Size of Your Breasts*

✦ 1983: *The Theory of Lengthwise Rolling*

✦ 1979: *Madam as Entrepreneur: Career Management in House Prostitution*

✦ 1978: *Proceedings of the Second International Workshop on Nude Mice*

✔ AUTHOR AND *NEW YORK TIMES* DISAGREE ON MEANING OF HIS BOOK TITLE: CASE HISTORY

When the national morning newspaper *USA Today* was started in 1982, journalistic critics referred to its trendy, highly readable format as "fast-food journalism" and nicknamed it "McPaper."

By 1987, after a tumultuous history and a furious struggle to stay alive, the paper finally fought its way into the black. The *USA Today* managing editor for cover stories, Peter Pritchard, wrote a book on that struggle in September 1987 and titled it *The Making of McPaper.*

"McPaper," Pritchard told this writer, "was a derisive term used by some journalists when the paper first came out. *Newsweek* had called it 'The Big Mac of newspapers.'

"I named my book 'McPaper' because the term had some sell to it. The people at *USA Today* also helped with the title.

"Alex James of the *New York Times* said the book's title mocks the newspaper's critics who nicknamed it 'McPaper,' but it doesn't. It just shows that we could take it."

---

*Not in anyone's winning column, because the publisher rejected the manuscript, but just as bizarre, was this title reported by a U.K. publisher in the July 17, 1987 issue of *The Bookseller: My Life with Woodworm: Forty Years with Wood Destroying Insects in Buildings.*

✓ MESSAGE TO SCOTLAND YARD CONVERTED INTO TITLE OF TONGUE-IN-CHEEK MYSTERY

When a body is found in the English village of Little Puddley, Scotland Yard is asked to "Send Bygraves," and that is how the title of the November 1987 mystery came to be titled *Send Bygraves.* The Bygraves in the book's title is a chief inspector of Scotland Yard who seeks out the murderer in a variety of disguises, and all in subtle but playful verse, accompanied by black-and-white illustrations.

The author of the tongue-in-cheek mystery is Martha Grimes, whose successful and acclaimed series of mysteries featuring Scotland Yard Inspector Richard Jury (where the tongue is not in the cheek) themselves follow an identifiable tilting device. All take their titles from the colorful name of a pub that figures in the story—such as *The Dirty Duck, The Man with a Load of Mischief,* and *I Am the Only Running Footman.*

✓ STORY BEHIND THE TITLING OF A PULITZER PRIZE WINNER

The Pulitzer Prize jury had nearly agreed on another book when the galley proofs of a forthcoming Macmillan book reached them.

As Macmillan Free Press editor Robert Wallace recalled: "One of the Pulitzer jurors read it and called the others, urging them to consider the late arrival. He said, 'It has winner written all over it,' and the other jurors read it, agreed, and awarded it the Pulitzer Prize for General Nonfiction for 1974 in a field of close to 200 candidates."

Charles Smith, vice president and publisher of Macmillan Publishing Company, remembered how the book's title was stumbled onto by pure chance.

Smith explains, "Editor Bob Wallace and I got two manuscripts from the author, Ernest Becker. They bore the ponderous titles of *The Natural Merger of Psychiatry and Religion: Kierkegaard, Freud and Otto Rank,* and *Marxism and Psychoanalysis: An Essay on the Merger of Science and Tragedy.*

"On the advice of another scholar, editor Bob Wallace blended bits and pieces of the two manuscripts into a single book. But the problem was what to name it. The answer was found in the book's preface, where the author said 'This book is about the denial of death' and we had our title, *The Denial of Death.*"

✓ HOW A TATTOO INSPIRED A TITLE

Publishing consultant Jack Howell recalls the details of how the most successful book of his publishing career came by its title.

He had contracted with two practicing psychologists in California to publish their book for Addison Wesley in Boston, where he was an acquisitions editor in the early 1970s.

"In the course of putting the book together," he recalls, "I had a meeting with the authors on a beach. In the news that day, there had been a story about a man who had jumped off the Golden Gate Bridge in nearby San Francisco, a suicide. When the body was recovered, it had been reported, there was this tattoo on one arm—'Born to Lose.'

"We were talking about the suicide story and the tattoo and it was jokingly suggested maybe it might make a good title for the book.

"'No,' one of the authors said as she looked at a little girl playing nearby with outstretched arms, 'I want *Born to Win.*' We all instantly agreed that that would be the book's main title." (The original manuscript title became the subtitle).

The 1971 book went on to become one of the all-time bestsellers, topping $3 million in sales (cloth, paper, and mass-market paperback) by the mid-1980s; it is still a brisk seller.

✓ FAMED NOVELIST'S TITLE GETS HIM IN JAM WITH HIS PUBLISHER

When the noted British novelist and humorist P.G. Wodehouse turned in a book manuscript titled *Money for Jam*, it was quickly turned down by his publisher as inappropriate. The title was a British slang expression for money easy to get or money on which you can count. The book subsequently was published under a title that was the American slang equivalent: *Money in the Bank.**

✓ TITLE SHOWN DIFFERENTLY ON EACH SIDE OF JACKET—FOR GOOD REASON

People who read books that have titles they don't want others to see often cover them with a plain brown wrapper. Here is one way this was avoided.

The publisher had issued a book with a title he felt might be offensive to the reader's boss if carried in to work, so he reproduced

---

*From: *Writing to Sell* by Scott Meredith, New York: Harper & Row, 1960.

the jacket copy on the reverse side of the jacket with a less offensive title.

The original title of the book: *How to Win Your Boss's Love, Approval...and Job.*

The title of the book with jacket turned inside out: *How to Win Your Boss's Love and Approval.*

✓ THREE TITLES: SAME CONTENT

The book, published by the Honolulu Zoo, bore on its cover the title: *Zoo Snakes of Hawaii.*

One review of the book praised it as being "completely devoid of zoological, grammatical, and typographical errors."

But those who bought *Zoo Snakes of Hawaii* found only 20 blank pages inside. There are no snakes in Hawaii!

Similarly, some years ago a European publisher issued a book titled *The Memoirs of an Amnesiac.* Its pages were blank.

When a New York publisher subsequently issued *The Nothing Book,* also with blank pages, the European publisher accused the American house of plagiarism. The accusation was promptly rejected with the response that blankness is in the public domain.

✓ SCI-FI TITLE THAT RESULTED FROM PUBLISHER'S TYPOGRAPHIC ERROR: A CASE HISTORY

One of the oddest reasons for a book title we encountered in the writing of this work was a typographic error. It had appeared in a printout of unfilled publishing contracts at Ballantine Books, a division of Random House in New York.

At one time, someone had signed a contract for a book with a working title of *Get Of the Unicorn.*

Through a typographic error, it was misprinted on the Ballantine list of unfilled contracts as *Get Off the Unicorn.*

When people at Ballantine kept asking editor Judy-Lynn del Rey about the book *Get Off the Unicorn,* she approached one of her science fiction authors, Anne McCaffrey, and asked if she could do something based on that theme.

The resulting McCaffrey book, a collection of 14 stories, was published by Ballantine in 1977.

✓ PHRASE FROM SONG CLASSIC PROVIDES TITLE, SHAPES REVIEWER'S THEME

When the highly regarded novelist Joyce Carol Oates titled her 18th novel *You Must Remember This, New York Times* daily book reviewer Michiko Kakutani (in an August 10, 1987, review) opened her rave notice with: "The title comes, of course, from the song 'As Time Goes By,' but there are no love songs and little moonlight in this book; only lots of passion, jealousy and hate."

Ms. Oates, who writes in what *Times* reviewer Kakutani called "powerful, meticulous prose," had chosen the words from the song classic for her book's title with the same meticulous care; the choice helped the reviewer open and shape the entire *Times* review.

✓ PATRON SUGGESTS JOKING NEW YORK CABBIE WRITE BOOK: HE DOES, WITH GUESS-WHAT FOR TITLE?

Jim Pietsch, a veteran New York City cab driver, over the years acquired the habit of asking his nighttime customers, "Heard any good jokes lately?"

Many responded and often would wind up trading jokes with the cabbie, who would record the good ones he heard while waiting at stoplights.

One of the cabbie's passengers, after trading jokes with him, suggested he write a book and gave him her business card. It bore the name Patti Breitman, then an acquiring editor at Warner Books.

Cabbie Pietsch followed her suggestion, and the book was published in March 1986. At the end of 1987, the $3.50 Warner paperback had gone through three printings and sold 50,000 copies. The title? What else—*The New York City Cab Driver's Joke Book.*

INDEX

NAT BODIAN is an independent publishing consultant. Until mid-1988, he was for 12 years marketing head for various professional and reference product lines and encyclopedias at John Wiley & Sons. His 30 years' book marketing and bookselling experience includes management positions for a number of leading scientific, technical, and scholarly publishers, and, early in his publishing career, as head of sales for The Baker & Taylor Company. He also enjoys an international reputation as author of seven book industry references including *Bodian's Publishing Desk Reference*, the classic two-volume *Book Marketing Handbook, The Publisher's Direct Mail Handbook*, and *Copywriter's Handbook* (for advertising and promotion of books and journals). He has been a speaker at numerous publishing group meetings and seminars and has written extensively for the publishing press, both in the U.S. and the U.K. He is currently a contributing editor to the *SSP LETTER* of the Society for Scholarly Publishing, a columnist for the *COSMEP Newsletter* and the *Newsletter* of The International Association of Independent Publishers, and a steering committee member of the Professional Publishers Marketing Group. He was a 1986 nominee for The Publishing Hall of Fame.